Praise for T.D. Jakes

"Jakes continues to deliver a message of hope and inspiration."
—*Booklist*

"Bishop Jakes is the quintessential leader with a heart for people in the now and an entrepreneurial vision for the church of tomorrow. Without hesitation I believe that Bishop Jakes is one of the best communicators in the world today. His ability to connect with people is God given, and I am personally inspired, encouraged, and challenged each and every time I am in his presence."
—Ed Young, senior pastor of Fellowship Church and author of *Outrageous, Contagious Joy*

"Bishop Jakes, my spiritual father, embodies God's limitless capacity to redefine, reenvision, and reinvigorate our journey in this life. He catapults those around him into newer and greater dimensions of self-awareness, and deposits deep wells of practical wisdom and spiritual inspiration from heaven into our hearts, minds, and souls."
—Paula White, Without Walls International Church

"Bishop T.D. Jakes is an anointed leader whose leadership, integrity, passion, and devotion transforms."
—Ron Kirk, former mayor of Dallas

ALSO BY T.D. JAKES

Reposition Yourself

Living Life Without Limits

T.D. Jakes

ATRIA BOOKS

New York   London   Toronto   Sydney

ATRIA BOOKS
A Division of Simon & Schuster, Inc.
1230 Avenue of the Americas
New York, NY 10020

First Atria Books trade paperback edition August 2008

ATRIA BOOKS and colophon are trademarks of Simon & Schuster, Inc.

Scripture quotations are taken from the *Holy Bible, New International Version*®. Copyright © 1973, 1978, 1984 by International Bible Society. Used by permission of Zondervan Publishing House. All rights reserved. Scripture quotations marked KJV are taken from the *King James Version*.

For information about special discounts for bulk purchases,
please contact Simon & Schuster Special Sales at
1-800-456-6798 or business@simonandschuster.com.

Designed by ISPN Publishing

Manufactured in the United States of America

10 9 8 7 6 5 4 3 2 1

The Library of Congress has cataloged the hardcover edition as follows:

Jakes, T.D.
 Reposition yourself : living life without limits / T.D. Jakes.
  p. cm.
 "Atria nonfiction original."
 1. Success—Religious aspects—Christianity. 2. Jakes, T.D. I. Title.

 BV4598.3.J36   2007
 248.4—dc22   2007005996

ISBN-13: 978-1-4165-4431-9
ISBN-10:   1-4165-4431-3
ISBN-13: 978-1-4165-4730-3 (pbk)
ISBN-10:   1-4165-4730-4 (pbk)

I dedicate this book to all of the many brothers and sisters who survived the horrible tragedies of Hurricanes Rita and Katrina. If anyone knows the power of repositioning yourself, it is you. I pray that you have a limitless life and achieve far beyond your wildest dreams. Just know that though many of us were not blown away from our base by the watery storms of a detectable nature, we have nevertheless often been uprooted by tempests that did not come from the sea. Therefore, let me broaden this dedication to include all survivors who dare with bold tenacity to reposition yourself. As one man who constantly faces changes and disappointments, I want to encourage you. Never give up, never give in, and, for God's sake, never give out. I believe that the best is yet to come.

Contents

Foreword by Dr. Phil McGraw

From our humble beginnings to our roots in Dallas and the deep and abiding faith at the center of our lives, I believe that I have some important life experiences in common with Bishop T.D. Jakes. We both have been blessed beyond all expectations. Yet, I think he would agree that our greatest shared blessing is that we both have been afforded the tremendous opportunity, through our respective platforms, to reach out to teach and inspire others to challenge and overcome their limitations while striving to fulfill their highest possible purposes on this earth.

Bishop Jakes certainly serves as a wonderful example to us all. This pastor, author, artist, entrepreneur, and philanthropist began his ministry in 1979 with just ten people in his West Virginia congregation. Today, he leads the Potter's House in Dallas, one of the nation's fastest-growing megachurches with more than thirty thousand members. Yet, that is just the home base for a spiritual outreach that now extends around the world. Through his broadcasts and missionary work, he is the spiritual shepherd to millions across the globe. Yet just as he did back in West Virginia, he continues to meet people where *they* are in their lives, bringing them a real and relatable message of the power of faith and hope.

With this book, Bishop Jakes builds upon that inspiring message by providing extremely useful tools and practical guidance to help real people, in the real world, to break through whatever barriers they may encounter in reaching for higher achievement—and the most fulfilling, prosperous, and authentic life possible.

Bishop Jakes believes, as do I, that the blessings granted each of us should be embraced, acknowledged, and—most of all—built upon with hard work and determination so that we keep growing and preparing ourselves as worthy recipients of even greater rewards.

It is an undeniable truth that one year from now your life will be better or it will be worse, but it won't be the same. No matter where each of us starts out on the socioeconomic scale, we all have the potential for prosperous and fulfilling lives if we take responsibility for our own successes. Bishop Jakes and I both strive to live by and teach that message. We both encourage you to stay on the path and refuse to accept limitations—either those imposed by others or those you place on yourself.

In the title of this book and throughout its pages, Bishop Jakes exhorts you to rise above your challenges, learn from your mistakes, build upon your blessings, and to continuously make adjustments so that you are always on track to serve your highest purpose.

Bishop Jakes and I agree that the measure of your success is not calculated by the material possessions you acquire but by the quality of the life you lead and the others you lift up and inspire along the way. The bishop serves as a model and a guide for that philosophy, and with this book, he both lights the path and ignites the fires within you.

PART I

The Sky's the Limit

INTRODUCTION

Back when I was a boy, if you had asked me what I wanted to be when I grew up, I would likely have responded, with a sheepish grin, "fireman" or "actor." Becoming an entrepreneur with a half-dozen diverse businesses, much less a preacher and pastor to a church of over thirty thousand members, would never have crossed my mind. Appearing on the cover of *Time* magazine and meeting with presidents, prime ministers, Academy Award–winning actors, and celebrated professional athletes, was outside my imagination as well.

My father, the founder of a large and successful janitorial business, hoped that I'd take over his company. My mother, an entrepreneur in her own right, probably thought that I would become a singer or dramatist. None of us envisioned me ministering to thousands of people around the world—from Africa to Asia, New England to New Zealand—or me publishing books and participating in film projects for the big screen.

My life has constantly changed as I responded to events, people, and opportunities. I have been divinely blessed by my Creator. I've also made deliberate attempts to grow, to position myself to receive, and to reposition myself to receive more.

I have failed and tried again, many times, before making significant progress toward my goals. My mistakes were also my lessons. I gained experience and did not allow my past mistakes to bind and gag me. The boundaries established in my own mind for how far I could go were pushed outward. I found the keys to living without limits.

Many of us attribute success or failure to fate or some external force. We believe that we have to be in the right place at the right time in order to achieve, much like winning the lottery. But success is a direct consequence of our wanting a more abundant life and working hard to earn it, like wading through the mud puddles of life toward the beckoning sea.

I believe that we are called by God to be the very best stewards of all the gifts, talents, and opportunities entrusted to us in this lifetime. The result is true prosperity, real success.

My deepest understanding of true prosperity came from an exercise in philanthropy to dig a well to provide water for a village in Kenya. My ministry team and I took a mission trip to see the people we had set out to serve. We escaped the concrete maze of our urban lives and ventured into the economic abyss of East Africa. We traveled by helicopter over the parched ground of the city of Nairobi to the barren terrain of the countryside, beyond the reach of electricity and indoor plumbing, where even such a basic necessity as clean water was a luxury. In an act of appreciation and celebration, a local woman, who had benefited from the work we had accomplished there, invited us to her home.

With her chestnut-brown skin, deep-set dark eyes, and jet-black hair, this woman, whom I'll call Jahi, displayed the regal poise of a queen and the humble hospitality of a gracious hostess. Her face bore the signs of living unprotected in a climate where harsh sunshine toughens the skin. Her thick body appeared quite strong, likely from carrying wood from miles away back to her home. Challenged to determine her age, I guessed that she might have been in her midsixties or more.

I was struck by the fact that this woman, who was rather short in stature, had built her house with her own hands, and as low-tech and humble as it was, she seemed every bit as proud of it as I am of my home with its many amenities. She invited me in with a sweep of her hand in a way that suggested that I was entering a grand estate—no matter that she had neither a doorbell nor a real door, only a woven drapelike fabric to allow in the breeze.

She described how she had built the home with dry branches gathered on the plains nearby and cow manure that she used as mortar to fill the holes and joints of the walls. All of the homes in her village were held together by cow dung. I detected a faint, earthy odor, likely all that remained from the pungent manure, now dried. Cows are the source and raw material for many of the necessary items in their lives. I sat on her bed made from the hide of a cow. Her dirt floors were swept clean. I could see the faint rake marks in them. She offered me a drink of milk that had been fermented into a yogurt of sorts, not recognizable as Dannon.

More than these details, I recall her sense of inner peace, how she bragged about God's ability to provide. She smiled brightly—revealing teeth that clearly had never been touched by a dentist—as she acknowledged how much prosperity she enjoyed. Had she been listening to the latest Tony Robbins tape? Or did she have riches that no accountant can measure that comforted her in a way that I knew nothing about?

Some are surprised that I comfortably sat in a house made of cow dung with my feet on a dirt floor. Many only know me by the sound bites they've heard about my success. You may see my life like someone who comes to the last few scenes of a movie, not having seen the beginning.

Jahi's little shack didn't look much different from the homes of some of my older relatives—for whom slavery was a recent memory and who swept and raked their dirt yards like the Kenyan woman did her floor.

I remember entering their homes on rickety steps beneath which canned preserves were stored. I recall that newspaper filled the holes of walls, blocking wind and even daylight from reaching inside. We did not have indoor plumbing either. We went down to the creek for water and to an outhouse rather than a bathroom. I know the humbling feeling of that experience in my own life.

It didn't stop there. I know also what it is to have my car repossessed, my children drinking milk provided by WIC, to make a game with my boys out of feeling our way through the house when the electricity had been cut off for nonpayment. I know what it is to count someone else's discards as my blessing and to do without altogether.

My visit with Jahi in a world where a goat is a luxury compelled me to revise my own definition of success and prosperity. I understood more than ever that prosperity is more than the trinkets of excess we use as icons of accomplishment and self-worth in our culture.

Prosperity is built upon progress, and progress is measured from the point at which we started. Many times in our culture we assume that we all compete on an equal playing field. That is simply not true.

As we were departing from Jahi's house, just as we lifted into the air, the clouds broke and released thin sheets of rain. Clapping, dancing, and smiling was the response from the village below. Our pilot explained that the rains are a sign of prosperity and great blessing. I smiled to myself, considering how often in my world the rain is viewed as an inconvenience, something that deters people from traveling.

Too often the term *prosperity* gets hijacked to mean nothing more than an elusive state of temporary bliss and positive karma. Certain extremists in the faith-based community teach that faith is only a matter of dollars and cents. They quote scriptures that promise great wealth. They don't emphasize the importance of a practical, pragmatic plan of a faith-with-works ethic, education, and economic empowerment.

Some among us manipulate Scripture to fit their own purposes and achieve personal gain. Others teach piety and asceticism and promote the idea that poverty should be worn as a badge of superiority, that it is somehow more godly to barely be able to feed your children than to be wealthy. This was and is the norm in some church communities.

My mother said that she studied by kerosene light, reading classroom assignments at the foot of a bed that she shared with five or six other children, all of whom walked miles each morning to attend school. Listen to her contemporaries reminisce and you'll hear one trying to outdo the other telling how poor they were.

I was raised in West Virginia, the second-most-impoverished state in the nation. I've gone up in the hills and seen poor people who were just as arrogant as their counterparts in other places who owned the latest Lexus. I've preached in churches where men who wore ties were disregarded while those who wore coveralls were welcomed. And I've preached to congregations where the opposite attitude prevailed. The healthy state of mind is somewhere in between.

Reposition Yourself: Living Life Without Limits is meant to give you the tools to help you succeed and be prosperous.

Success equals good grades if you're a student taking a midterm exam. It is closing a deal if you're a CEO. It is the purchase of a home if you're a single mom now renting. It could also be a Mercedes to park in front of your condo or a donkey to ride to an open-air market.

I hope to also give you some tools for coping with people—and their numbers are great in our society—who have contempt for your success. America is one of the richest nations in the world and yet so many of its people feel disdain for the wealthy. Some also feel disdain for the poor. We think of ourselves as middle class and entitled to look down our noses both at someone we think is a welfare mother, and at someone we think is a designer-clad lady living in luxury. Neither attitude is justifiable.

God blesses His people—all of us. Faith is the substance of whatever it is that we hope for. The important thing is that we teach that faith is connected to good works and responsibility. Otherwise, when we teach that faith is all that is necessary, we teach a belief in magic. Isn't it time for you to direct your hope toward building your dreams instead of waiting on your dreams to build themselves? As we look at various areas of your life, if you're willing to reposition yourself, then truly the sky's the limit!

one

The Courage to Confront—Facing Your Own Indifference

Then you will know the truth, and the truth will set you free.

—John 8:32 (NIV)

In just a short time I will have been on Earth one half century. I've already started celebrating this benchmark. So many memories. When this milestone birthday came up recently in conversation, a friend asked me, "What words of wisdom have you garnered? What would you do differently and what would you say to those who feel that they only go around once and feel powerless to correct what may be perceived as less than glowing results?"

I thought before I answered and then said, "There is nothing worse than reaching the end of your life and wondering what could have happened, or should've happened, but somehow didn't happen." The sad memories of a lost opportunity have made many people bitter the rest of their lives. Often it is not the fatigue of the Olympic competitor that is debilitating as much as it is the feeling that if he had lunged farther, or pushed harder, he might have been holding the golden cup of victory as opposed to the bottled water of defeat.

None of us welcomes regret. We want to live to the fullest, spiritually, financially, and even relationally. Yet we often settle for less than the best life we could live. Lulled into sleep by a sense of apathetic compliance, we accept as limitations situations that could be transcended. Are you tired of living from paycheck to paycheck? Do you feel like you're stuck in a job while wishing you had a career? Hold your breath while credit cards clear? Do you grow weary of those closest to you feeling as if they cannot get in touch with who you really are? No one knows but you the extent to which your public success masks private failures. Do you want more out of this next phase of life than what you have now?

Most of us do not want to wander aimlessly, taking life as it comes. We want to take charge of our destiny and see goals accomplished progressively, according to a plan. There are things in our lives that limit us.

You can only correct what you are willing to confront. Now, I have to admit, confrontation isn't always something that I enjoy. But I have learned over the years to say what has to be said and face what has to be faced.

Many choose to live in a perpetual state of denial rather than do the hard work that is needed to confront issues, weaknesses, and inconsistencies in themselves and others.

Do you have the courage to face the dark, silently sinister enemy that may be lurking inside of you? Do you have the courage to confront yourself? Don't worry, I am here with you. For the purpose of healing and not hiding, take a heart-to-heart look at some issues that may be stopping you from reaching your goals and living your life to the fullest. Things can turn out the way you want, if you're willing to hear the truth.

Stop the Madness

Perhaps you're familiar with the process known as intervention. Frequently used for cases of abuse of alcohol and drugs as well as for addictions to unhealthy behaviors, intervention is a valuable tool for helping the person who has destructive behavior see the patterns of his life and their effect on those around him. While an individual will deny the problem and resist assistance from friends and family who attempt to aid him one-on-one, the intervention brings the entire circle of key relationships abruptly into the addict's presence, often using the element of surprise. Surrounded by those who know her best, the person is forced to look at her addictive or compulsive behavior and examine her life, perhaps facing the truth of it for the first time. As each person shares what she sees and feels about the deterioration of her relationships, it becomes next to impossible for her to deny the problem. Here are the people who love her the most, all sharing similar observations, concerns, and solutions for the problem that has taken over her life.

Interventions can be extremely effective in helping addicts accept help. When conducted in a spirit of love and encouragement, the intervention can save the life of the addict and reawaken her to a world filled with opportunities for health and wellness. It is simply amazing how love can win out over obsessions, addictions, and adversities. Love can be a tremendous deterrent to destructive behavior; it gives the individual the support she needs to change her life. Though the Bible says that love is as strong as death, it is stronger than debt, divorce, depression, or any obstacle.

This intervention will not consist of a normal group of teary-eyed, emotionally charged individuals. You're likely not addicted to drugs, and not overtly destructive, but there has been an erosion of growth and wholesome abundance in your life. Today we are staging an intervention to get you out of this rut!

Who is joining us? We could certainly have your spouse or partner testify; they have witnessed the consequences of your apathy. Your kids could speak up as well. Perhaps your best friend. Your siblings. Your parents. Coworkers. Your pastor. Your apathy has affected each of them, dulling the edges of your talent and ambition and hiding the best parts of yourself from them. Many people in your immediate circle may be watching you live your life in ways that are far beneath your potential and character. Ask those people in your immediate circle what they've noticed and witnessed in your life.

But for now, imagine you just got home from work, and as you walk into the house, you unexpectedly find, sitting around the table, your friends who cared enough to come to this intervention to get your life out of the dismal realm of the ordinary and into the spectacular realm of extraordinary possibility thinking. Supposedly to support you, but more accurately, as we are about to see, silently enabling you. These friends today are confronting you. Are you ready?

The Distant Dreamer

Beads of perspiration appear on her forehead as Dee opens her mouth to speak. You know Dee. She is the dreamer who always stayed near you in the early years. She is like the voice in your car's navigational system, the one who used to navigate your decisions. Lately, she has been quiet, silent, as you make wrong turn after wrong turn, delaying your arrivals and hindering your progress. But now, with a nervous edge, hating that she has been selected to be the icebreaker, with a parched throat and a crack in her voice, she begins the process:

"It's been so painful to watch you settle for less and less in your life, working a job beneath your talents and capabilities, accepting the roles that others assign to you, giving up the creative pursuits that once fueled your ambition. I'm the part of you that longs to be all that you were created to be, the dreamer inside you who loves to look ahead and aim for the top.

"I remember so many big plans we had back in the beginning. We knew there would be obstacles, but we were young and had set our eyes on the stars. We were going to go beyond what you had growing up, to have a fuller, richer, more liberated existence. You had so much imagination and such a vision for where you were going and how you were going to get there. You could see yourself in your mind's eye, growing, reaching, and attaining a life of satisfaction, contentment, and joy."

It is obvious to the others waiting to speak that your walls of defense are as high and formidable as the walls of Jericho! Dee knows it, too. But with a strength that only comes when we finally share the truth, she releases her concerns. She now realizes that she should have said this to you years ago instead of silently letting you go this far off course.

"Do you know how hard it has been for me? I mean, I love you, and I hate to watch your life get harder and your ability to see the pinnacle that was once your destination and motivation seem to disappear in the daily fog of working, living, and then working some more." Looking you in the eye for the first time, she continues: "I watched as your circumstances got tighter and choked the wind out of your lungs. Disappointments set in, followed by losses and realities that threatened your hopes for ever experiencing a different, better life that would allow you to be who you really are and live out your God-given purpose. Those around you did not encourage you. I tried to come around to nurture and support you, but you pushed me away, becoming more and more distant and detached.

"Instead of fighting to keep the fire inside you alive, you let the embers die by becoming addicted to a life without dreams, without hope." Almost venting she continues, "After all I did for you. I brought you through the hard times. Don't you remember? I was there when life was bad. Did you just forget all of that? You locked me up in the cellar of your soul and placed me on a starvation diet. All I hear from you is complaints about who 'wasn't there for you' and who didn't treat you right. But I was there," Dee Dreamer continues.

"Or I would have been if you had let me! Over time you've become cynical and negative, subtly bitter and internally angry, looking for targets to blame—your parents, your lack of opportunities, your family. People don't know it because you are masterful at covering up your true feelings. I know this is not the life we dreamed of for you when you were younger. This is not the love you wanted, the house and career you wanted. I know better than anyone sitting at this table how you dreamed of more than this. You were meant to be a high achiever. My God, you have gifts you aren't even touching, much less using. This ordinariness doesn't become you, and I had to say something today! It is beneath you and what you were created to be. Your answers, your power, is in your dreams!"

Reaching out to you with a warm hand and a now wet face, Dee gently touches your shoulder and says, "I need you—no, we all need you." The others sitting at the table give a warm nod. There is the sound of a few quiet sniffles. Dee Dreamer finishes her appeal with these final words: "Instead of being fully alive to the possibilities of the future, the pursuit of the dreams that God has planted like seeds in your heart, you have resigned yourself to an existence without dreams, a parched desert place of indifference where nothing can grow.

"You can't go on this way—it's killing you. Fight for the dreams that were once such a vital part of your life. Don't give up hope. Throw off the limits that other people, organized religion, and many other forces may have placed on you. Like a butterfly emerging from her cocoon, you must discard the useless husk that you continue to let cling around your dreams. I know it is not too late. You can use all that you have been through as wind beneath your wings. Come on, it's time to fly!"

The Listless Lover

Each person looks around the room, wondering who will be next to speak. L Lover speaks up and says, "I want to tell you something." L Lover had been loving, optimistic, romantic. The giver. "You know as well as I do, love gives and lust takes. You have replaced love with lust; you take but you stopped giving. Lately my attempts to engage your heart have been thwarted by regret and sabotaged by bad memories. These memories are what you use to justify being emotionally detached, lustful, and selfish. The only reason I agreed to speak today is that I want to love you actively again."

Everybody at the table listens as he speaks. Each takes in his words, which reflect the true substratum of the issues they all have had with you. They all know that true love has been absent from your life for a while. They know you have been faking the feelings that used to be genuine. L Lover clears his throat and says, "Our relationship with each other has become so strained I don't even know where to begin. Whether you think of me as your heart or desire or love, I am the part of you that longs to love and be loved, to be in a healthy dynamic relationship with another caring person. Like our friend Dee Dreamer, we started out strong and were inseparable.

"We shared the fairy-tale dream of finding that special someone who would get us, who would see us as we really are and love us unconditionally. We thought we had found that soul mate a time or two. I stayed with you throughout those first few tender, sweet, and painful relationships. We thought we were in love and maybe we were, but for various reasons, the relationships didn't work and you were alone again.

"And then, over time, you pushed me further and further away. As you've gotten older and continued to struggle in your search or watched a once special relationship stagnate, I've grown tired. And instead of seeing what you're really worth, you start selling yourself off for so much less than you're worth. Low self-esteem pushed you away from me. What I could have fixed, you hide. Lust for power, for money, and even for sex has taken away your passion. You used to really be there, in the moment, present in the conversation. You were open and warm and giving and sincere. Now you're concerned with who has the best job or who can get you where you're trying to go.

"Look at you now. I see you faking your interest, distracted by what you need. You stopped giving, so you stopped getting back. You can't sow indifference and get back affection. Forget about the relationships that went bad or had issues. Don't lose sight of the loving person you were meant to be. You stopped loving the idea of love. Your authentic self is camouflaged by a self who has no feelings. Do you know that living inside of you is like being trapped inside of a mannequin?

"You've accepted status quo security and predictability over what you and I both know you long for deep in your heart—passion, spontaneity, desire, and intimacy—don't get me started about when you quit hoping for intimacy! Those have all gone by the wayside. Getting ready to be intimate with someone now is like October thirty-first. You dress for Halloween! You start the relationship like it is trick-or-treat night. Neither the tricks nor the treat are what they would have been if you had knocked on the door with a come-as-you-are openness. That is why you keep getting tricked. It is that layered costume you wear to protect your heart. That costume has imprisoned you! Take off all of those silly masks and be yourself!"

A nervous giggle breaks out in the room and then a somber sobriety sets in again as he continues. "The relationships you do have seem flat and unfulfilling. You don't communicate. You don't dare hope for romance. You're jaded and cynical about everyone's ulterior motives and the way they ultimately betray you. You're angry at your heart for longing for love. You blame the other gender for being so different, so fickle and untrustworthy, so unavailable.

"But listen. If you keep pushing authentic love away and settling for your apathetic lifestyle of one-night stands and dismissal of those in your life who could love you, then you will never know the intensity of pleasure for which you were created. And I'm not even talking about sexual expressions here, although we both know that plays a part.

"You deserve to love and be loved and to face the fears and disappointments that haunt you, and move on. It's time to love boldly and passionately, to bring romance back into your life, to hope again, as Dee already said, for a good person in your life who could love you for who you are."

That is when you speak up. You have had enough of this confrontation intervention mumbo jumbo. Annoyed and embarrassed, you reply, "I am not addicted to anything! I am in control of myself and my circumstances. I did all right for myself without any of you. I am still okay by myself. I am not addicted to any of you or anything else."

L Lover and Dee Dreamer speak up and in unison they say, "You are addicted! You are addicted to apathy!"

L Lover continues: "You stopped caring. You stopped dreaming and believing."

Dee Dreamer says sadly, "You are hooked on indifference. No real passion burns inside you . . . not like it used to . . ." She sighs. "Not anymore."

Manny the Manager

A new voice enters the conversation. "Your addiction to apathy has affected everything. It has affected your business—your finances are going to hell! And don't even get me started on your credit!" His anger boils as he says, "You are just letting things go. You don't handle your business anymore. You won't face up to issues and they are not getting better. They are getting worse."

Manny had held his peace as long as he could. He seemed annoyed, almost belligerent. Everyone at the table looked at him, surprised. Dee Dreamer pats Manny on the shoulder and tries to calm him down. He is angry because you won't allow him to confront you about this apathetic attitude that has ruined your business opportunities, carjacked your credit rating, and murdered chances you had to be further along financially. Manny is a number cruncher, you know the type—a computer geek of a guy. He is not tender like LL or diplomatic like Dee. Manny is a guy who deals with facts and figures.

He continues: "You are getting older, and if you keep spending like this . . ." Manny shakes his head and then says, "I am in your life to ensure that when you are old you have a retirement. I am in your life to make sure that you do not keep going on emotional buying binges. I watch you buy what you want and then struggle for what you need. Honestly, it makes me ill. I wanted to set your finances on track so you could pay for your children's education or have money to invest in a home or that little vacation spot you saw in the Bahamas. If you had followed my plan, you would be shocked how much further you would be today. If twenty years ago you had invested the price of a Happy Meal every day, you would have been wealthy by now!

"But it is not too late. That is why I am here today. You have to stop this apathy. You seem to have caught a spendthrift virus or maybe a financial flu!

"Maybe it is because you and L Lover are not getting along. I notice when your love life isn't right, you compensate by over-spending. Or maybe it is because you and Dee Dreamer aren't working things out. You seem not to have any capacity for delayed gratification. If you would just wait, you could have so much more of the good life and reach your dreams. In the absence of the dreams Dee talked about, you spend. When things aren't going right with L Lover, you stop managing your business and spend too much of your time, and I daresay your money, on things that are not valuable. Your priorities are all out of whack! It affects you and me.

"When they called me about this meeting, I was the first one to show up. I was here early." He reaches into his briefcase and starts throwing unpaid bills onto the table. "This has gone to a collection agency—a collection agency! It is a forty-two-dollar bill. Now there's a thirty-five-dollar late fee attached. That's ridiculous! You and I both know you could have paid this. But you aren't handling your business!"

Manny looks at you and growls, "I bet you don't even know your credit score. How can you correct what you will not confront? You won't look into getting out of this rut. What I am trying to say is simple. If you stick your head in the sand and ignore things that you have the power to change, you can't blame anyone when they don't turn out right!"

He takes a deep breath and calms down a bit. "I am here today because I care for you. I am here today because I believe in your dreams. But most of all, I am here to try to get you to wake up from this apathetic sleep you have been in and get a handle on your life. Listen, I know you have faith and I know you believe in God. But God helps those who help themselves. Or maybe I should say faith without works is dead. You can't just *pray* about business. You have to *do* something. Doesn't the Bible say that a blessed man is one who 'whatsoever he *do*eth shall prosper'?

"Listen, God can't bless what you won't do. You haven't been taught correctly. Prosperity doesn't just come from giving an offering. It's good to be a giver. But you must also be a thinker, a planner, and a worker." Manny sighs, glances around the room, and then says, "I am not trying to get you to be rich. I just want you to have the best and most positive life you can have with the gifts and opportunities God has given you. I don't know if you have any will to fight this. But it is not too late to turn this mess around." He looks down at the financial statements, disconnected-service notices, student loans, and foreclosure notices flung all over the table. "If you fight back you can beat this addictive destructive habit of apathetic indifference."

The Blinded Believer

Before you can catch your breath and let Manny's words sink in, Bee jumps in. "I am your spiritual self, the one who relates with God and seeks His truth in all areas of your life. Your addiction to apathy has starved you spiritually, seeking to fill the place only God can nourish with material items—expensive clothes, new cars, and other toys. But we both know that there's something so much deeper and satisfying that you crave. The contentment that comes from fulfilling your God-given destiny. An awareness of the many blessings that He daily sends your way.

"But you don't expect much from God because of your painful past wounds; life seems so unfair. You are disappointed with pastors and churches that appear hypocritical and focused on judging you. You idolize the material in the hope that it will fill a spiritual void. God breaks through and wants you to dream, to reposition yourself like Zacchaeus the tax collector climbing the sycamore tree to see the Savior. But you numb out, tired and exhausted, preferring to go through the motions rather than really engaging in a relationship with your Creator, the One who wants to comfort, heal, inspire, and motivate you to new heights.

"If you truly want to break through your addiction to mediocrity, your recovery must be spiritual. It doesn't necessarily involve going to church. That is good, but without a personal relationship with God, churchgoing is empty. Focus on what your soul hungers and thirsts for: to relate to God."

Bee looks you directly in the eyes and shoots her questions like bullets into you. "Do you want a meaningful life? Do you want to experience a peace that passeth all understanding and an abundant life of purposeful joy? Then it's time to fight to win your life back. To rekindle the hunger for the holy in your life and seek out God's destiny for you. Renounce the troughs of pigs' food and return home to the Father who's waiting to run down the road to meet you.

"God will guide you, but only you can take the first step on the exciting journey known as the rest of your life. Aren't you tired of the slop for which you've been settling? You may have squandered your resources so far, but God delights in providing His children with what they need when they rely on Him. It's time. It's time right now. I have been praying for you. I have been praying for you while you drove to work. I have been praying for your mind, amidst the clutter of day-to-day demands. I have been praying about your instabilities, infidelities, and insecurities. God said, 'Return unto Me and I will return to you.' God is just beneath the distractions in your life. He loves you even when you are wrong and ignore Him. Can you imagine what it would be like if you really got together with God again?"

The group huddles around you and joins hands. Bee lifts her voice, then Manny, followed by L Lover and by Dee Dreamer. They each pray a prayer of courage and relief for you. They ask for divine guidance and assistance in breaking through your addiction to apathy and bringing you back to your senses.

As troubled and disturbed as you are by their confrontation, you know that something has to give. Something has to change in your life. You can't hold back your emotion any longer. And as their voices fade, you whisper, "I'm ready."

Do-over vs. Make-over

These characters exist in all of us. I have had to face them myself in my life. These characters are the voices of reason that we often muzzle rather than listen to. But if they could intervene and confront us in love, we would all be better people. There is more life in your life. You could be more fulfilled if you took courage to make some minor adjustments and repositioned a few sadly neglected parts.

Did you ever play baseball or kickball as a kid and get to have a do-over if you missed your swing or your kick? We all wish we could have a do-over for the many mistakes and missteps we've committed. We can't. We must live with the consequences, the mistakes. But let's not do so without questioning what we can learn and how we can grow from them.

You can't have a do-over but you can reposition yourself and have a make-over. It doesn't involve plastic surgery, a radical diet, or a new wardrobe, although by the time you're done, you may be inspired to do all three! No, the kind of make-over I describe in the pages that follow involves throwing off the shackles of your addiction to apathy and embracing the tools needed to reposition yourself for a life of freedom and enrichment.

If this feels selfish or self-absorbed to you, then realize how many other lives are affected by your well-being. One of the key reasons why an intervention is often successful is it produces an awareness of how your behavior hurts those around you. Any time you're not focused on what matters most because you're allowing yourself to be distracted and numbed by some feel-good urge, it's hurting those around you.

If you know it's time and you are more than ready for a major life change, your recovery has begun. Your desire to change will only fuel your fight to reposition yourself into who you were meant to be.

If you're dissatisfied with your life, long for much more, and feel the desire to take some risks and make some changes, but those impulses are countered and blocked by your past disappointments, by the safety of your present status quo lifestyle, and by the uncertainty of your future, you are on the fence. You are flirting with the tragedy of a life wasted and regretted. Get off the fence and onto the road of recovery through repositioning.

If you are so deeply embedded in your addiction to apathy and mediocrity that you don't see what you're doing to yourself, afraid to let yourself hope, committed to busyness so that there's no time to think and reflect on what your life means and where it's headed, it's time to stop. Don't be afraid to want more and go after more. Winds of change are blowing your way.

You can have a better life. The question is: Are you willing to fight for it? Like an alcoholic recovering from the throes of his addiction, are you willing to fight the urge to settle for less and to endure the hard work required to reposition yourself? If the answer is yes, then turn the page.

two

Beating the Air—
Fighting Failure
with Your Eyes Open

I therefore so run, not as uncertainly; so fight I, not as one that beateth the air.

—*1 Corinthians 9:26 (KJV)*

In many ways the impetus for this book started several decades ago in a schoolyard brawl. I have never forgotten the invaluable life lesson I learned from a bully named Harold. I was a third grader at the time, and he was a year ahead of me. One day after school we had words about something—funny thing is, I don't even remember what it was! But I do remember like it was yesterday the impact of his chubby fist connecting with my head. He basically beat the ever-loving taste out of my mouth!

We had traded words back and forth after the bell rang but waited until we were almost home to actually scuffle. We punched and rolled, swinging fists like prizefighters on Pay-Per-View. Yet only one of us was connecting his punches! I wish I could say that he didn't win, or even that it was a close call and I wasn't sure who won. (I tried to save face when I got home by pretending it was a close fight.) But I knew from the look on my brother's face that I had sustained a fairly uncontested "beat-down"!

The main problem was that I was fighting with my eyes closed. If I could have just opened my eyes a little more often, I might have fared better. Harold beat me so badly that when my father came home that evening, he got down on his knees and gave me my first lesson in self-defense. Dad, who was my superhero at the time, had me demonstrate my stance and technique. After observing me for a moment, he chuckled and said, "Son, your big mistake is that your arms are flailing out there like you're imitating a windmill. And your bigger mistake is that your eyes are closed like you don't want to watch someone kick your tail!"

The Fight of Your Life

Now that I'm grown, I have to admit that Harold, my schoolyard Goliath, really did beat me pretty good. It was my first taste of many bitter hard-fought battles, not necessarily with my fists but with my mind, heart, and spirit. I learned from that fight a fundamental principle that must be our starting point if we are to reposition ourselves amid the ever-changing battles of life. If we are going to throw off the limitations of past failures, we must look for opportunities to learn from our losses.

Although I absorbed a lesson in self-defense at the time, it wasn't until years later, when I read the verse at the beginning of this chapter, that the lightbulb of understanding over my head exploded into fireworks of life application. Writing to the church in

Corinth, the aged and sage apostle Paul penned a message from which you and I can gain insight into how we can reposition ourselves for the victory that God intends for us.

You cannot win against that which you will not see and confront

An ostrich style of fighting with your head buried in the sand is highly ineffective! When we "beateth the air," as Paul phrases it, we swing empty punches that expend energy without effecting change. Beating the air is not like beating the opponent! You should have seen the force with which I hit the air in my fight with Harold. If only one of those blows had connected, I would have knocked him out cold. Instead my lip was swollen up like a balloon filled at a water fountain!

No, we must be strategic and deliberate. Our punches must connect. We must fight strategically for the prizes we long to enjoy. We must invest our energy in direct connections to our goals. Often well-meaning people say to me, "You deserve the success—you work so hard." I understand what they mean. They are comparing me to people who do nothing and expect everything. But it's a mistake to believe that hard work always yields great results.

Effort doesn't necessarily mean you are effective

Unfortunately, in an effort to raise children who were not lazy, our parents taught us that hard work was equal to better living. Most of our parents and grandparents spent their lives in tough-task jobs during the twentieth-century industrial age when productivity centered on efforts and energies, not strategies and structure. Could it be possible that our parents prepared us for a world that passed with them? Could our twenty-first-century techno age require us to reposition ourselves for a new way of thinking? Have we unwittingly limited ourselves by clinging to Mama's ideals and Daddy's work ethic?

Stagnation is the danger of traditional thinking. The wisdom of our elders could have been great for the times when we heard them. But a progressive and continual reassessment will avoid the pitfall of applying an antiquated ideology that causes us to expend effort but doesn't get desired results.

To survive in the highly technical and postindustrial age that you and I live in today, we have to update our personal philosophy. Our parents and their ancestors have laid a great foundation, for which I am eternally grateful. But it is dangerous to try to build additions to a house that was constructed for a climate very different than the present one. Yet subconsciously we often stay with the inherited framework and never make any advancement into contemporary progressive thinking that will increase our effectiveness.

When Hard Work Is Hardly Working

I know many people who work like mules but see very few results. They unknowingly limit themselves by maintaining self-imposed beliefs that perpetuate exhaustion of resources without ever increasing productivity. I have been around friends who were far busier than I but far less productive. Their cell phones interrupt our lunch. They drive down the road giving instructions on their Bluetooth and seem busier than the control tower at O'Hare Airport in Chicago. They are well intentioned, doing what they perceive is necessary to realize their aspirations.

In fact, most of them are filling a variety of roles in an attempt to multitask and increase proficiency. These small-business owners may actually be the chief cook and bottle washer. This pastor may be leading the choir, picking up his members, and counseling inner-city teens. This working mother may be chairing the PTA fund-raiser, soliciting new accounts for her employer, and scheduling an appointment for the carpet to be cleaned. These people compose intimidating lists of Herculean proportions, racing from place to place and responsibility to responsibility only to check off the next item. They pour out their hearts only to see dwindling, dwarfed impact of their many efforts. What would we say to the student who studies hard, disciplines his behavior, but still finds it difficult to pass the test? Something is wrong with his study habits!

Can you relate? Does it feel like you're running in place on the treadmill of activity after activity, chore after chore, duty after duty? Are you expending constant motion only to stay in place at best? Have you boxed yourself in by what you feel you "should do" to achieve success?

Unfortunately, so many of our attempts to live successfully can be similar to my pathetic attempt at fighting Harold! Here's the problem: *I was in the fight but I wasn't aiming at anything.* There I was sweating and cursing, screaming and swinging, while he was still punching me in the eye and the lip. Angrier than ever, I became even more misguided in my efforts to fight back!

Likewise, life can beat you up and circumstances can keep you down even as you struggle valiantly and courageously to stay in the fight. I was angry enough to win. I was strong enough and big enough to win. But no matter how committed I was to my cause, my efforts were poorly guided. Are there areas in your life where you are fighting like I did? Could your busy schedule be full of empty punches that don't connect with anything of substance? Are your eyes closed to learning from past mistakes instead of repeating them?

Periodically, all of us face those seasons of life that are difficult to survive. Often they are brought about by circumstances seemingly out of our control. A mere illness can go far beyond doctor's visits to a battle of will and faith—not to mention finances—that's tough for anyone to endure. A brief time of unemployment is not necessarily a big fight but only a temporary situation that everyone finds themselves facing at some point. But if this temporary phase turns into a three-year sabbatical from a pay stub, it may be the battle that tries the soul and exhausts the financial reserves, leaving our families bewildered, our marriages strained, and our confidence shattered. Any one of these calamities and countless others can leave you feeling forlorn and hyperstressed.

Our greatest sorrows and most intense struggles emerge from the places that once brought us joy. There is nothing as beautiful as a lovely wedding, nor anything as traumatic as a soured marriage. How many times have I seen a mother weep with joy as her newly birthed bundle is placed in her hands. She cannot imagine that these salty tears of jubilation may, in seventeen years, turn to bitter frustration when she wakes up to find that little Junior has taken her car without permission and has disappeared again.

Like a baby developing from stage to stage, life has a way of presenting us with unexpected changes. One moment a job is a wonderful blessing, and a few years later you find yourself standing before an arbitration board with frustration that you never saw coming. One doesn't have to live long to know that even a wonderful relationship, business or personal, often presents challenges that can quickly turn into a conflict resembling the battle of Armageddon! I have seen children who were once confidants and trusted allies turn on their own parents and try to destroy them. I have witnessed lovers who couldn't breathe without hearing each other's heartbeat later abhor the sound of the other's voice. Even a trusted friend can end up a formidable enemy.

Keep the Change

We may not see the sweet become the bitter until the taste fills our mouth and our eyes are watering with the pain of the transformation. The only thing certain about life is that it will change. We're forced to keep the change in our lives whether we want to or not, realizing that the best of situations can turn on a dime and become the worst crisis we've faced. So many of life's hardships derive their power from the unexpected timing of the punch that catches us off guard.

Although all of us face these trials, it seems that some people have a secret edge that enables them to withstand the vicissitudes of life. Their counterpunches are swift and well aimed, accomplishing more in one blow than twenty swings by someone else. These people seem to bounce back from all that would drag them down and impede their progress. They are not exempt from life's heartaches and headaches, though it often appears that they have some free pass that enables them to bypass problems like an executive-club flier expedited in an airport.

Yes, we all struggle, day in and day out. However, some people simply manage the challenges better than others and are thereby able to expend their energies on winning rather than merely enduring the undetected Scud missiles that come out of nowhere, threatening to detonate their careful plans with the shrapnel of the unexpected.

No matter how faith-filled, how financially responsible, how politically correct you are, or how congenial you may be with others, you will inevitably find yourself from time to time facing moments that threaten you like a terrorist attack. These private struggles haunt us and leave us with a secret angst that hangs around like hot spicy foods in a system that has no gall bladder!

These troubling issues stagnate in us, refusing to be digested as they move into our emotions, constipating our creativity and distracting our energies to no end. Many of us have bought into the myth that simply having an upbeat attitude or a faith-filled philosophy somehow exempts us from challenges. But, my friend, it simply isn't so.

The good news, however, is that we can convert the storms of opposition into the wind beneath our wings. We can use these experiences in which we're pushed to the wall to break through barriers and expand our playing field. We can move beyond the limits of our past mistakes, transforming folly into wisdom, frustration into fuel, and denial into the detonator of explosive change. The failures of the past can become battle scars that toughen your hide and make you more resilient and resourceful moving forward, if you will only allow those tender wounds of regret and disappointment to heal.

How can we make this transformation? How can we aim ourselves strategically in order to accomplish the most effective actions and move toward a life without limits? What can we do to change our lives?

The process begins with understanding how relentless and tenacious we must be in order to prevail over the adversity we confront. There is a mind-set of the champion that gives him an edge. It is his refusal to accept average or ordinary that puts him in a place of unprecedented distinction. In fact, there is a discipline and training that forever positions the gladiator as the winner he was meant to be. Once he has been programmed to succeed, he will ultimately rise to his highest and best self because he has been trained to win, conditioned to prevail, and called to be a conqueror. He has been positioned to be a winner, and even if he loses everything, he has that nebulous, seemingly indefinable gift of landing on his feet in shoes with silver linings. You know, those people who can turn chicken manure into chicken salad!

Running Scared

In the same letter to the Corinthians that I mentioned earlier, Paul uses a metaphor about athletes who train for a race, disciplining their bodies for the purpose of attaining a crown, which in his day was a simple wreath of leaves for the winner.

> Do you not know that in a race all the runners run, but only one gets the prize? Run in such a way as to get the prize. Everyone who competes in the games goes into strict training. They do it to get a crown that will not last; but we do it to get a crown that will last forever. Therefore I do not run like a man running aimlessly; I do not fight like a man beating the air. No, I beat my body and make it my slave so that after I have preached to others, I myself will not be disqualified for the prize.
>
> 1 Corinthians 9:24–27 (NIV)

How much more, he asks, should we train and discipline ourselves to attain what matters most? Paul knows that success—whether spiritual, physical, or financial—is intentional. No one trips across a finish line in the Olympics and says, "Oh, wow! How did I do that?"

Successful runners train diligently, carefully control their diet, and awaken early each morning to run sprints with only the rising sun there to greet them. These winners train for the day of competition, and when it comes, the sheer joy is no doubt intoxicating, seeing that what they intended to achieve has now been accomplished. Completing, let alone winning, the race is an extremely gratifying feeling that is preceded by years of preparation that may have started when the athlete was a child.

I remember once chatting with Deion Sanders, the famous National Football League cornerback and Major League Baseball outfielder whose versatility as a professional athlete kept him in demand for over a decade. He was an exceptionally skilled runner whose strong legs and lightning stride positioned him for an extremely impressive career in professional sports. He helped lead two different NFL teams to Super Bowl victories and was voted Defensive Player of the Year in 1994. One of these teams, the Dallas Cowboys, signed him to the most lucrative contract a defensive player had ever signed at the time.

Deion was as intimidating on a baseball field as he was on the gridiron. (In fact, he is the only man to have played in both the Super Bowl and the World Series!) Most often his legs ran him onto the Cincinnati Reds field, where he played for four seasons (1994-95, 1997, 2001). It was during one of his many stints with the Reds that he and I began to build our relationship. One day when he was sharing some of his history with me, Deion mentioned that he started running as a child because he lived near a cemetery. He said that as a boy he was spooked by the headstones and the morbid feeling the graveyard inspired. To avoid this unsettling feeling, he would run as fast as he could to get past the cemetery on his way home. There, with no one in the grandstands to cheer him, he found his legs to run. Though this activity wasn't part of an orthodox training program, it still helped prepare him for his life's career.

Although this early experience might have been accidental, Deion made it clear that the development of his skill was definitely intentional. Many times we may seem just to stumble into our talents, but developing that talent to its promised end is always done on purpose. What started for Deion as running scared in the graveyard was developed fearlessly in the gym, on the track, and ultimately on the field of every major stadium in the country. As he signed multimillion-dollar deals for his expertise, won dozens of awards, and now has retired to a posh mansion and a career as a sports analyst, he could say that he stumbled into his gift through that graveyard experience. While the graveyard may have revealed what it was he had inside him, it was the hard work and conditioning that fulfilled his potential and launched him as a world-class athlete. It's a long way from a little boy running from a ghost to a man sweating and leaping across a goal line! In between those two points, his success was intentional.

Degrees of Success

Obviously, a large part of being intentional about fulfilling your potential relies on education. However, I should warn you that finding your gift is more than getting a degree. While this varies from field to field, many experts estimate that over 50 percent of people end up working in areas other than the one for which they have earned a degree. Education gives you information on a subject and a degree is often based on the number of credits we have. We end up completing a degree only to find out that we do not like actually working in the area that we enjoyed studying. Maybe we should have students spend a year as an apprentice working in the area for which they want a degree in order to help them determine what they really want to do.

Such an apprentice system reflects one of the fundamentals of persevering to succeed: most of our life's energy is spent in trial and error. I thought I wanted to do this the rest of my life, but now

I don't. She thought she wanted to be married to him, but she now guiltily realizes that she thinks she's made a big mistake! Even the brightest, most intelligent people make early decisions that they later regret. You must realize that no mistake—no matter how large, costly, unacknowledged, or painful—can cost you the power to change your life. You may have to start with baby steps to redirect your life and get going in the right direction, but it can be done.

Part of your education—and by this I mean truly learning from your past mistakes—requires assessing correctly what you have in your personality that can empower your arsenal of weaponry. If you have the tools in your heart that match the information you have in your head, then you can begin to find the most powerful areas for their convergence. The combination of a focused mind and an impassioned heart can be so helpful in determining what we are really meant to do with our lives. Like Deion's graveyard experience, we may need something to jolt us into motion, but cultivating a talent and attaining a goal are efforts of intentional focus.

Taking Inventory

If you've ever worked a retail sales job, then you likely endured an end-of-the-year inventory analysis. Every retail business, from shoe stores to supermarkets, has to assess what it actually has in the store compared with what the records indicate should be in the store. Similarly, if we are to find this convergence of mind and heart, talent and tenacity, then we must assess what we have in our personal warehouses.

For you see, the first step in fighting the good fight is arming yourself with an accurate analysis of your purpose and dedicating your efforts to cultivating the area of your gifting. Fulfilling your purpose or purposes for living (some people have more than one and may explore them simultaneously, or decide at some late date to go after a dream that was put on hold for a while) begins by identifying the area that gives you a sense of satisfaction and well-being. You must then have the courage and tenacity to see that abstract fantasy become concrete reality in your life.

That might sound simple, but in reality most of us are forever living our lives dancing to the beat of someone else's drum. I have had to learn as a parent that I can influence but I cannot control my children's choices. At times I have sincerely but wrongly tried to live my life over vicariously through my children. And I'm not alone—many are the parents who have taken their influence to an extreme and put their children in a lifelong prison of trying to live up to a mother's or father's expectations. Or what about those of us who allow our competitive tendency to compel us toward what we actually do not want just in order to prove a point to someone else, as if their opinion were the barometer of our accomplishment?

As the national trend toward changing careers, on average, once every seven years continues, it seems likely that we're not just getting bored and wanting a new challenge. So many people, from doctors to lawyers, sales reps to CEOs, teachers to talent scouts, tell me that they went into their field to prove how successful they could be to someone else. Then they wonder why they feel empty, exhausted, and overwhelmed!

No, we must be honest with ourselves and listen to that voice within us, pay attention to those items that make our mind race and our pulse skip, and investigate the requirements for building our dreams. If you are reading this and beginning to squirm, then I encourage you to examine what's making you uncomfortable.

There is no shame in being a janitor—I know because I watched my father labor beyond his physical capabilities as one—if you do it with pride, dignity, and a sense of fulfilling your true purpose. So the first step in taking inventory—and we'll be coming back and developing this further in later chapters—is to be real with yourself about who you are and what you really want. It's definitely much easier to fight if you know who you are and what you're fighting for!

Adopt to Adapt

Now, to be sure, victory is not accomplished without conflict. Change is inevitable, and if we are going to be adept at fulfilling our dreams, we must arm ourselves with the right tools in order to achieve each task along the way. My mother used to say all the time that anything worth having was worth fighting for. I believe that. I believe that winners are fighters who do not quit. Now, if you are in a fight to realize a dream or fighting to maintain the dream, I encourage you to fight effectively and not hysterically!

Business leader and author Jim Collins, whom I recently had the privilege of meeting, provides an exceptional illustration in his bestselling book *Good to Great: Why Some Companies Make the Leap . . . and Others Don't.* Collins compares two grocery giants, A&P, the largest retailing organization in the world in the 1950s, and Kroger, a small value-based chain of supermarkets also thriving in the fifties. As technology began to progress in the tumultuous sixties, both companies, very traditional in approach, saw that the world was changing around them. Each company conducted research, built expensive test stores, and hired expert analysts to forecast the future.

They both reached a similar conclusion: because of the way the world was changing, convenience was paramount. People would want to do as much one-stop shopping as possible: food, toiletries, pharmacy items, prescription drugs, and so on. In a stunning lapse, A&P took this information and basically ignored it. Kroger, on the other hand, acted on it and implemented the "superstore" strategy that we now take for granted. By 1999, Kroger had become the leading grocery chain in the United States, generating profit eighty times that of its onetime competitor A&P!

Now, A&P fought hysterically but Kroger fought effectively. Often our inability to adapt to changing needs, assess the business climate, or utilize past data before investing in whatever it is we hope to achieve leaves us fighting like a fool rather than with the skillful accuracy of a professional. As we discuss repositioning yourself, I want you to be a marksman and effectively hit the mark by not fighting as one who beats the air! I want you to pace yourself and adapt to changing times and waxing and waning tides.

If you truly want to live to your full potential, then you can no longer, like an A&P, ignore the signs of the changes around you. Because you're reading this book, you're probably already aware that you're not living as effectively as you'd like. Perhaps you've even been talking—with your spouse, a coworker, a friend—about changing your life in some dramatic ways. But it's time to quit talking and start walking!

In the fight I lost with Harold, I made the most noise, but he got in the most licks. I was intimidating, but he was effective. Thank God for my brother and father, who took me in hand and began to give me a few lessons on effective fighting. It was easier to learn how to fight and win on the school bus than it was in the more challenging world of adult life! If you learn on each level, you can then reposition yourself to fight more effectively on the next.

I challenge you as we close this chapter to consider whether or not your fighting techniques are producing the desired effects. Are you defending yourself in a way that is proactive and productive? Or are you closing your eyes to the reality in front of you and swinging in the dark? Is your energy directed strategically and focused deliberately on maximizing your time and resources? Bottom line, are you experiencing the joy that comes from living a life without limits?

It's a process for all of us, my friend. So regardless of where you may find yourself, I know that I can offer you some progressive steps for prospering from the inside out. But you have to be willing to rethink how you go about running the race and pursuing your goals. You have to be willing to revise your ineffective attempts and reposition yourself for maximum impact. Are you ready? Then get out of the box and into that sweet spot in life that only you can fill!

three

Lost and Found—Finding Your Present Location by Knowing Where You've Been

And the LORD God called unto Adam, and said unto him, Where art thou?

—*Genesis 3:9 (KJV)*

Past failures and present predicaments can sometimes make us feel as disoriented in this maze called life as the characters on the TV series *Lost*. The passengers of Oceanic Flight 815 experienced an explosion in midair that sent them plummeting down to a deserted island. As the castaways fight for survival, they encounter others' personal agendas, hidden dangers, and mysterious characters at every turn. Just like life! On the island they have to ask themselves the intriguing question "Where am I and how do I get out?" All of us have been stuck at some point and wondered if we would ever be able to move on and get out.

Like our friends on the *Lost* series, we all lose our perspective when we do not have the navigation we need to find out where we are and what we need to fix the problems that have occurred. You don't have to be a pilot to understand the potent power of navigation. Cars are now being manufactured with navigational systems loaded into them. They save us hours on a trip as they help us avoid needless delays by simply telling us where we are in relation to where we are going.

If we are to overcome our failures and disappointments in life, we must develop our own navigational system. While such a system only provides location and direction—not fuel, not the power to steer, not the ability to choose the destination—such information is nonetheless crucial for navigation. Similarly, if you are trying to locate yourself, keep reading. I have something to tell you.

Fate or State?

The question I had to ask myself in those times when I was sinking in a quicksand of debt, sitting in the dark with no electricity, stuck at home with my car repossessed, and faced with a hungry family and no means to feed them was: Do I accept this as my fate or simply as a temporary state? If it is my fate, then I'm finished and I should give up.

I answered that I was in a state, one that I could fashion, transform, and resist. I did not succumb to despair, but rather persevered.

When I think of this process of choosing state over fate, I think of the life of Joseph in the Bible. He goes through stages. He feels lost in the prison of despair and has to find his gift in order to change his life.

Joseph was the second youngest of a dozen brothers and was his father's favorite. Gifted with prophetic dreams, Joseph is hated by his brothers for this talent and the future his dreams portend. They attempt to murder him but can't go through with it, instead selling him as a slave to traveling foreigners, who take him into Egypt. His sincerity of character and prophetic talent earn him an important role as the house leader for Potiphar. But when Potiphar's wife takes a lustful liking to her husband's employee, Joseph resists her advances only to find himself accused of rape and imprisoned.

Talk about life being unfair! Our boy Joseph has faced just about every trial imaginable, his only apparent crime being that he is a gifted man of integrity. But his ability to interpret dreams soon reaches the ears of the pharaoh, and faster than you can say reversal of fortune, Joseph finds himself second in command of the entire country. He prepares for the upcoming famine and lives to see his family, whom he forgives and embraces, reunited. (For more details of Joseph's life, see Genesis 37–50.)

Joseph was bound by his circumstances. But he overcame them by using his gifts. He transcended from the mundane to the miraculous. It is so easy to become engrossed in one circumstance and lose sight of the limitless power that lies within what we have been given. Like Joseph, it's vitally important that we all recognize how tremendously gifted we are. It is through understanding the power of your gifts that you can escape the prison of despair. Imagine what would have happened if Joseph had stopped using his gifts just because he was in a prison. He would never have been released, he would not have prepared Egypt for the impending famine, and countless lives would have been lost.

Do you find yourself in a situation that could be improved by using more of the resources you have at your disposal? Joseph found himself incarcerated until he discovered a new way to apply his abilities. He re-created himself in a time of need to provide a service. He repositioned himself from convict to commissioner. He couldn't accomplish this, though, before he realized the position he was in at the beginning. You have to identify who you are and where you are in order to find your gift, your voice. You must speak up and gain your power to move beyond the present prison even if it involves confronting a situation that has left you feeling degraded, demeaned, uncertain, and irrelevant.

Vision, so crucial to this process, is often one of the first powers we lose when despair sets in. Several years ago I met with a gentleman who was running for president in his country. He was discouraged by lack of finances and felt defeated. I spent a few hours motivating him to believe in himself and his abilities so that I could see him achieve his full potential. You cannot achieve what you cannot conceive. He thought his problem was lack of finances, but I knew that it was lack of vision. He couldn't recognize where he was. Initially, I think he wanted me to be a campaign contributor, but what I gave him was better than money. I sat with him and helped him locate himself.

My friend the candidate thought he was stuck when in fact he had everything he needed. But when we are too close to a situation, we will often misdiagnose the problem and feel defeated when we could actually prevail. In his case, he was pursuing something that really wasn't in his heart. Sometimes we end up going somewhere because of someone in the backseat of the car. In effect, we who are driving have given control to the passenger. Take the wheel of your life now and go where you are meant to go rather than allow your passengers—mothers, spouses, neighbors—to control your destination. Success is not achieving what someone else wants you to achieve. Success is discovering your gift and using it.

You can determine where you are by evaluating what you have accomplished. How does it compare to what you dream of achieving? A goal is to get what you see on the inside to happen on the outside. You will know you have it when there is no difference between what you see when you sleep and what you wake up to. In short, I am telling you it is possible to live your dream wide-awake. The distance between what you dream and what you see is achievable.

"But, Bishop Jakes, I am *so* far away from what I dream," you say. So was I, my friend, and even now, I have to occasionally recover from a wrong turn. Even with a navigational system, you can still make a wrong turn. The great thing about navigational systems, though, is that if you do get off track, it will recalibrate itself based on your wrong turn, redefine where you are, "forgive" you for being off track, and set you back on the right path. I have never had the system say, "You fool, why did you make that turn in the first place? I told you not to do that!" Yet most of us spend precious time beating ourselves up for what we did wrong rather than recalibrating ourselves and moving ahead.

Now you must understand that positioning requires understanding where you are and measuring it against where you are going.

Exact Coordinates

While there are many tools to assist you in locating and repositioning yourself on course, one of the most helpful that I've encountered emerged from one of my peers' teachings. Years ago I was in a meeting with Ed Cole, a life coach who led what remains an incredibly powerful discussion with a men's group. He shared principles that I would like to break down into five stages of progression in any relationship or situation. These principles, though not infallible, may serve as catalysts to help you better locate yourself in your career, marriage, or other aspect of your life. They can assist you in determining the exact coordinates necessary to rechart your route toward a life without limits.

For you see, one of the first questions recorded in the Bible continues to serve as a North Star as we navigate our way through the dark forests of life. After Adam and Eve had eaten of the forbidden fruit, recognized their nakedness, and clothed themselves with fig leaves, they hid, out of shame. The Lord seeks them and asks, "Where art thou?" Obviously, He knew the answer to His question without having to ask it, so clearly He asked for the benefit of His listeners. Having disobeyed God, Adam and Eve had their eyes opened to a new reality and had to reassess who they had become and where they were. Basically, like each of us, Adam and Eve became caught in a riptide of change and were forced to reposition themselves.

Like our original parents, we, too, must face the changing landscape of our personal gardens. Therefore, it is essential that every man or woman answer the proverbial question "Where art thou?" For men in particular it is often difficult to ascertain where we are, as we often tend to focus on what we do and what we have, which might actually camouflage a deep sense of isolation hiding beneath the facade of degrees, stocks, bonds, church-membership growth, or whatever you deem as a measuring stick of achievement.

For men and women alike, this self-analysis is not easily conducted in a society that seldom asks where are you, but largely focuses instead on who are you and how you measure up against others. But if we are to reposition ourselves for a life without limits, then these stages provide an invaluable assessment tool. These five stages and my interpretations and elaborations are as follows:

1. **Revelation.** This is the stage where we discover our career, our companion, or some new opportunity of significance. Men are incredibly visual beings. We are inspired by what we see. In order to become more, we have to be exposed to more. The more we see, the more our strength to become more is released. I often quote the adage "If you can see the invisible, you can do the impossible."

   In Scripture, revelation often literally means to "unveil." The most powerful relationships we can have are with those who help us to see what we didn't see before. A church or school or even a friend who unveils possibilities and potential becomes a limitless resource to those of us who are upwardly mobile. Often we meet someone or attain a position that unveils a new piece of the puzzle of who we are. Like eyes opening, we become blatantly aware that there is more to life than what we have seen before. Whether it is the unveiling of a lovely young lady met on a train ride or the article we read at the newsstand of a powerful new trend in marketing and real estate, these events open our eyes to possibilities previously unseen or unnoticed.

   In this stage what is unveiled to you is a challenge you accept as falling within the scope of your own sense of purpose. If you stop here, then you are doomed to remain simply a voyeur in life. Regret comes to those of us who saw opportunity but lacked the power, the will, and the intestinal fortitude to go beyond voyeurism to the next stage of action!

2. **Inspiration,** the second stage, provides more of the fuel that is used to ignite the passion needed to overcome the inevitable

struggles that stand between us and our next conquest. This second stage expresses a heart condition that's indicative of our new interest; it would be the equivalent of a letter of intent in a business proposal. In a relationship, this is the moment of impact when you decide to take it to the next level. This is the stage when a guy asks for a phone number, or it may be the stage when he gets his feelings hurt.

In your career, this is when you decide to commit more deeply to one area of specialization or even one company. It may be the point when the résumés are passed or interviews set up. Or perhaps it's the stage when a bid is made on a contract, when a point of entry is offered.

Regardless of what's at stake, this is an important stage, as many people lack the passion to go after what they have realized in the first stage. These perpetual procrastinators never seem to gather the momentum necessary to achieve because they lack the inspiration to overcome adversity. This is why many motivational speakers receive such a warm reception in our country. Businesspeople, professionals, and even spiritual people have begun to identify the significance of motivation, which is the ability to inspire persons to achieve their dreams. It doesn't give you the dream; it empowers the dreams that have been revealed to you in the previous stage. Inspiration is often the catalyst of action.

3. **Formalization** develops after an inspirational stage that has ended in an affirmative answer. In other words, "You're hired!" Or, "Yes, I want to be your spouse!" It may even be a letter from a university acknowledging your acceptance. It is the point where the issue has evolved to the degree that it requires a more formalized commitment.

Uh-oh, there goes that word that makes the heart flutter and the pulse go weak. This is the stage where the dates turn into wedding plans. This is the stage where the two-week notice must be submitted and a commitment to go forward is inevitable. My mother would have said, with far less tact than I am using here, "Pee or get off the pot!" You have sat here long enough contemplating the next move; it's time to act.

This is the point where you sign the deal, and it is now a formalized part of your life and existence.

Many women say they've known too many men who failed to reach the third stage. Inevitably, the sky grows slightly darker and the feelings become less romantic and more practical as we get into the nuts and bolts of becoming an "institutional entity." This is not about romance; this is about who pays the bills, who takes the children to school, and who washes the car. When a person doesn't make it to the third stage, he becomes trapped on a perpetual treadmill of repeating the first two. Like a failing student, he is left back in school, repeating a class but never passing it. He is forever dating but never commits to a formalized loving relationship. The woman keeps asking him almost like God did, "Adam or Richard or Demetrius, where are you?" I will tell you where he is. The man is stuck in stages one and two!

Some are always starting new vocations, new careers. They have great ideas but no follow-through, give a great interview but make terrible employees. They are stuck in a remedial class of life, always repeating the course, making the promises but never the commitment. They beat the world at coming up with limitless possibilities, but they never attain realities because they lack the ability to make it to the third stage of formalized commitment! Let's face it, there are benefits that cannot be attained without commitment.

In fact, the fulfillment of formalization is determined by your personal ability to commit to and engage in what you dreamed about previously. This is not a question of whether you have the skills, nor is it simply a matter of possessing the dream. Rather, this is more centered around the crucial question *Does the dream possess you?* Does it possess you enough to sacrifice to make it functional and formal? In employment, it requires the hard work of fitting into the culture of a company and integrating your skills into a new environment. You are in, you are there, you are part of the company, part of the institution, which brings us to our fourth stage.

4. **Institutionalization** is the point where the trouble often begins. When things become institutionalized they can lose their savor and become mundane. Subtle deterioration begins. Enthusiasm wanes. All of us have noticed couples who used to beam at each other, totally uninterested in dinner, gawking across the table in anticipation of each other's next word. But as the years go by, they sit across from each other, looking at each other less and less, the conversation stale and the passion evaporated. Soon all that's left are the sad memories of a feeling gone cold.

Or haven't you worked with people who dropped themselves off at the office like a FedEx package—one that slowly revealed itself to be oversize and empty, with no ideas, creativity, or interest? They are present solely for a paycheck. They are so institutionalized that they are about to become crystallized. Which, incidentally, is our next stage.

5. **Crystallization** occurs when deterioration has taken its toll. At this terminal stage, there is little left that functions the way it once did. All are present and accounted for, but no one is glad that the other is there. In a marriage, it is the feeling that often precedes a call to a divorce attorney. Most people do not fall out of love as much as they fall out of passion and lose the enthusiasm for relating to their spouse. And then they feel guilty because they love someone they can no longer live with. The relationship has become crystallized into a hard, brittle shell of what it once was.

Most people do not know how to rebound from this fossilized stage. However, if we can take the old love life into a new environment, we often can reignite it. Or perhaps the company offers a new position that starts the engines of creativity flowing again, and we go back to the first stage. I have learned that even great employees need new challenges to reignite their passions and enhance performance. This perpetual cycle affects our finances, as we often lose financial motivation when we lose a sense of creative purpose and flow.

There are many casualties of a crystallized entity. In a marriage, it may be the children. In a law firm it may be a court case. In a business, it may be the difference between an IPO and a privately held entity not evolving for lack of creative ideas.

What I'm trying to do is scream into your ears, "Warning, warning, warning." Get away from the crystallized stage because it will make you give up something good. It's a season that seems like a death sentence.

All of us go through these stages.

Back to one

Unfortunately, some of us get stuck in stage five and never get out, while others keep going back to the revelation stage and re-creating themselves over and over again. The early church fathers kept returning to Jerusalem whenever things went awry; it was their way of going back to stage one again. Congress goes back to the Constitution to get back to one. Company staffs review their mission statement in an attempt to return to their core values and objectives. Pianists rehearse scales as a warm-up for a complicated piece. Or if they're really stuck, they pick up a guitar! A new instrument is sometimes required if we are to escape the crystallized music of the past and create a new melody.

If you are stuck in stage five, as we all inevitably are from time to time, go back to one and get a new and exciting revelation and repeat the process over and over again. I see women who get married after being widowed, while others say there are no good men. The former are women who, like certain companies, keep reinventing themselves and reigniting themselves by taking up hobbies, going back to school, placing themselves in new environments. They remain interesting and passionate by going back to stage one for repositioning. Like the mythological phoenix rising from its own ashes, they are reborn again and again.

Change the music and change your dance. Do what you can to open yourself up to a new revelation of the stalemate you're in. Maybe you pay off old debts. Maybe you begin to date again.

More than money can buy

If we are to avoid stagnation, then it's important that we do not allow ourselves to reduce prosperity to money alone. Often money is only a measure of how comfortable our surroundings are; it is not truly an expression of personal contentment and self-realization. That's why so many people work so hard to earn more money but find themselves exhausted and empty because they never have time to enjoy it. Progress apart from purpose ends in arrogance.

I am simply saying that you can be rich and miserable. You can be a financial giant and an intellectual dwarf, emotionally bankrupt and void of enthusiasm. You and I have both seen wealthy people miserable as they discover that luxury items and posh vacations are not a replacement for human attention, enthusiasm, and love.

Success can often make the successful crystallize and become out of touch with their passion for a given pursuit. Their primary focus on acquiring wealth or success in a single area or business often causes myopia, and causes their internal worlds to shrink along with their hearts. Most successful individuals discover that they must unleash their passion in other areas if they are to remain engaged with life and avoid boredom of the soul. They need a fresh challenge, whether it is the philanthropic initiative of a Bill Gates or a former first lady running for the Senate. Or consider Emmitt Smith, who managed to reposition himself before millions of television viewers on *Dancing with the Stars* by transforming his agility and moves on the football field into a graceful performance on the dance floor. We all need ways to get back to one and re-create ourselves.

Do you know where you are in these five stages and what you need to do to move forward? Or maybe the better question is *Do you understand that all of life from summer to winter, from seed to harvest, from menstrual cycles to menopause, is just an expression of this one truth?* Life is a series of cycles. As you know, a cycle is really nothing more than a circle, so turn around, circle back, and get back on course. Only, this time, let's take it to the next level—a level without limits!

Understanding this "seasonal" truth, the meaning of which we will unpack more in a later chapter, will help you avoid depression as you realize that wherever you are, this, too, shall pass. If this is a good season, don't become overconfident and think you won't have a challenging one at some later point. If it's a crystallized stage, don't allow any so-called therapist to give you a prognosis of death. You can break out of the crystallized stage, and it begins by knowing that it is simply a stage along the way. Now let's explore how to lose the place where we are stuck and get on with the cycle of life.

Have It Your Way

My son is taking night classes and working during the day. My daughters are in college, too, but they are going full time. Each has chosen an option based on the variable that is unique to his or her situation. I want you to list the options available to you and tailor a plan to fit what is best given the options you have left. If you start looking with a positive attitude, you will find that there are a lot of ways to get back home from the Land of Oz. Clicking your heels may only be one way, Dorothy.

There are many navigational systems in life. Sometimes a mentor is a navigational influence. Sometimes parents can be navigational influences. Prayer can assist with navigation. Most of us are affected by many contributors. They either contribute to our success or they contribute to our dysfunction. But none of us got where we are, good or bad, by ourselves. Someone helped you get there and someone will help you get out.

A drug dealer isn't born the way he is any more than an astronaut is born an astronaut. Someone helped him get there. Rapists had help getting there. Scientists had help getting there. Navigation is influenced by environment. As a child, you could not control your environment, and likely suffered some pressures and parental issues that hampered your development. But the good news is that as an adult, if you want to change the destination, you can begin by using the navigational system you have.

I challenge you to begin to design an environment that is conducive to where you are going. Most of us are stuck because we live in an environment that is based on where we have been. We may even cling to places from the past and "retro" relationships that retard our progress. A healthy environment must include people who will support and encourage you, challenge and stimulate you. If you are to reposition yourself successfully, then you must begin today to build a support system that is based not on what you did wrong, but on where you intend to go.

Do you have the right people around you for where you are going? Identify those who are navigationally right for you and build those relationships. Approach them with humility as well as confidence and let them know they are significant to your success by what you say and how you behave around them. The wrong way to approach them is from a place of neediness. Rather, ask yourself what you have to offer them, how you can make their lives better. People love to be around others who give to them and feel better about giving to those who are themselves generous.

Whenever I'm visited by African leaders, they always come with a gift. As you know, Africa is a continent that is composed of many countries, and within those nations, many tribes. But giving gifts is common across national and cultural lines. At first I found it confusing, since in our country we typically show up for appointments and meetings empty-handed. However, the Africans always bring a welcoming gift to those with whom they are meeting, re-gardless of what they expect the meeting to bring them. Being from agricultural backgrounds, they know that you cannot reap where you have not sown, you cannot harvest fruit if you have not planted seeds and fertilized the ground.

four
Against the Odds—
Overcoming the Fact
That Life Isn't Fair

Masters, provide your slaves with what is right and
fair, because you know that you also have a Master
in heaven.

—Colossians 4:1 (NIV)

You don't have to be an oddsmaker in Las Vegas to know how difficult it can be to sustain hope in the face of life's many adversities. No one is immune to the virulent attacks of illness, divorce, unemployment, or loneliness. I'm not above it, you're not above it, and the many people you view as successful—whether talking from your television screen or walking down the aisle at your church—are not above it. We all, each one of us, daily deal with the sharp collision of our external realities and our internal aspirations. The result is often a wreck of major proportions that leaves us limping through another day, sore and disjointed, more exhausted and discouraged than we can imagine.

Whenever I speak, whether in ministerial or motivational settings, the refrain that I often hear from individuals before, during, and after the event is this: "Bishop Jakes, I believe in what you're saying. I know that God can do the impossible. But I also know the way life works, and it's not working so good for me right now. It works for most people. But you don't know what I've been through, what I'm up against." And then the person often commences to share a heartfelt litany of trials and tribulations involving everything from childhood abuse to physical illness. Regardless of my brother's or sister's explanation—and believe me, I take each one seriously—the end result can be summed up by the dull and defeated look of desperate desolation flickering in their eyes like the last ember of a dying fire.

These people always feel so alone in their unique and individual struggles. Many of them may know, as I do, that statistically they are not alone, and in fact constitute a large segment of the population of the suffering. But a statistic means nothing until that number has a face. In this chapter I want to address those of you who feel like you are on your last legs, barely standing. Those of you who picked up this book skeptical that I had anything to say that you hadn't already heard and dismissed as too idealistic, too religious, or too difficult to believe.

My message is simple. Life is not fair. You will have to overcome odds that may be stacked against you. But you can change the outcome of your life if you will refuse to give up hope and each day refine your vision of who you really are. It will require a new way of seeing.

Paint by Numbers

You see, a statistic means nothing until it affects you or those you love. Like one of those paint-by-number kits that I used to receive from my artistic auntie each Christmas, the facts of our life situations rarely translate into a real portrait until we apply color and dimension. In fact, the hard odds against our success can seem cruel and insurmountable unless we are exposed to those who buck the odds. If we settle for the paint-by-number pictures of who we are, then we miss the true artistry, the individuality, and unique stylistic beauty of a Pablo Picasso or Ellis Wilson.

In fact, many times the so-called statistical evidence and empirical odds are nothing more than misperception and someone else's spin. For a number of years there was a great outcry that there were more African-American men in prison than in college.

This was largely based on the results of a study from 2001 conducted by the Justice Policy Institute, a nonprofit organization in Washington, D.C., entitled "Cellblocks or Classrooms?: The Funding of Higher Education and Corrections and Its Impact on African American Men." This study reported that there were 603,000 black men enrolled in college in 2001 and another 791,000 imprisoned. This conclusion received considerable media attention, journalists decrying the outrage of such a travesty of human potential, with which I heartily agree. It's a tragedy any time a man or woman has his or her life diminished by incarceration when they could have been fulfilling their potential in making constructive contributions.

However, the results of the study were found to have included *all* black men who were incarcerated that year, not just those of college age, usually defined as eighteen to twenty-four years old. Once the numbers were corrected and a more thorough comparison made, it was clear that the number of brothers in college exceeded that of those behind bars. Yet in an oddly prophetic irony, that finding has slowly eroded and now there are indeed more black men of college age in jail than in the classroom, according to the most recent U.S. Department of Justice data.

My point here is that you cannot base your life on the so-called odds of your demographics, no matter how specific, accurate, or inclusive they may or may not be. Numbers can always be manipulated to support, refute, or justify most any position. The key is that you do not allow others' perceptions and probabilities to define and decide your destiny. You are the only one who controls the ultimate odds against your own likelihood of success.

Before you tell me that I'm out of touch or idealistic, please understand that I speak from an awareness of the same harsh realities of history as you. As a black man reared in the sixties, I know all too well the harsh realities of covert and overt racism. I grew up in environments that were filled with racist behavior. I know firsthand the cold blight of an unwelcome learning experience. I also understand that people who were not victimized in that way see any discussion along those lines as whining and simply say, "Get over it," much like a man telling a woman that the pains of childbirth are not that bad. In reality, you cannot understand a pain that you have never felt. But there is a despair in our country that makes the headlines only during times of unusual crisis. The poor and disenfranchised have no car, no plane tickets, no options, but the worst part is they often have no voice. In spite of the easy silence that covers such trauma, it is real and it does exist. This stench of unfair circumstances goes far beyond the water-drenched streets of New Orleans that followed in the wake of Katrina. It is manifested in a bewildered, distraught people who have lost hope of beating the odds.

And while numerous factors contribute to this situation, there are a handful of issues that consistently eclipse the rest: the lack of parents who value education, the lack of male role models, lack of self-esteem, lack of funding for teachers and facilities in elementary, middle, and high schools. So many children can't see any legitimate way out of the hood except by becoming a basketball star or hip-hop artist, leaving many to look to illegal and dangerous methods of escape—gangs, drugs, and other criminal activity. If we are to buck these odds, then we must be willing to emphasize and consistently demonstrate the incredible life-changing power of education. We must be willing to expose these children to examples and role models of success to show them who they can become.

I understand that academics have not been well marketed to inner-city kids who have seen more bling-bling in choices other than an education. It is hard for an academic to compete with the sexy images of entertainers whose big payoff is displayed on the TV screen every night. Kids do not see university professors driving through town with beautiful girls on video shows. I am not saying that they *should* see that. But there must be a way to market education and success that attracts the struggling and not just the starchy! Nothing in the world these young people see invites them to education. They are not being informed and consequently they have decided that education is not for them. But they are wrong!

One such success story is that of my friend Terdema Ussery, who serves as president and CEO of the Dallas Mavericks as well as CEO of HDNet. Now reporting to billionaire entrepreneur Mark Cuban, Ussery had earlier been president of Nike Sports Management, where he worked with Nike founder Phil Knight. Ussery graduated from Princeton (where he now sits on the board of trustees), and earned a master's degree from Harvard and a law degree from the University of California at Berkeley. He's been profiled in

Sports Illustrated, the *Wall Street Journal,* and *USA Today.* He is consistently ranked in the *Sporting News* annual list of the "100 Most Powerful People in Sports." Sitting on several charitable boards at both the national and community level, Ussery takes pride in giving to others.

To meet him and to read his stellar credentials, you might think that my friend had been born into a life of privilege, wealth, and intellectual elitism. However, he grew up in the Watts section of South-Central Los Angeles. While he enjoyed a good family life, with both parents present at home, he rarely saw his father. Not that Ussery's father shirked his responsibilities; it was just the opposite. His father was so busy working two jobs to support his family that he never made it to his son's basketball games, band concerts, or track meets. It wasn't until Ussery was an adult and had the privilege of caring for his father after a critical injury that the two connected deeply.

In addition to his father's absence, Ussery was consistently exposed to riots and gang warfare in the neighborhood. It was the mid-to-late sixties and racial profiling, police brutality, and political corruption raged all around him.

His community offered him a grim picture of what to expect in life. But thanks to parents who valued education, he discovered a narrow escape hatch that permitted his vision to exponentially expand beyond the oppression around him. He watched friends from the playground become all-star athletes, and while Ussery liked sports, he realized early on that education was his ticket out. He escaped becoming a statistic by owning his desire to be more than what he saw around him.

Field to Factory

Unlike Terdema Ussery, it's so tempting, as you grow up, to view the fences around you as impenetrable walls. Even if you're able to see through your fence to the swimming pool in a neighbor's yard or the beautiful rose garden across the street, you may still feel like you can never scale the wall to experience such a setting for yourself. But to accept such a limited vision is to settle for less than that for which you were created.

If you are black, you must realize that despite the seeming unfairness of your life circumstances, you have freedoms for which your ancestors labored and died trying to provide. Their enslavement provided the human capital to build this country's wealth during the agricultural age. They were robbed of the benefits of their labor, pouring out their life's blood for the bloated wealth of white property owners. It's an understatement of gross proportions to say that this was unfair. But still our forebears pressed on, despite the injustice, and despite the apparent futility of their efforts to effect change.

After the Emancipation Proclamation, our forefathers and mothers contributed mightily to the prosperous age of industry, working in sweatshops and factories to earn a meager wage for their families. While the yoke of slavery was technically removed from their shoulders, the burdens of racism, prejudice, and intolerance continued to weigh them down. Nonetheless, they persevered into the second half of the twentieth century under the inspirational banner of leaders such as Rosa Parks and Dr. King. Our community elders believed that their hard work was worth more than the sore muscles and modest paycheck they earned.

And their efforts were not in vain. Today we have seen considerable change, as evidenced by the likes of Terdema Ussery, Senator

Barack Obama, media mogul Cathy Hughes, Secretary of State Condoleezza Rice, and Academy Award–winning actor Denzel Washington. But there is still work to be done and we all know that many of the issues faced by our ancestors continue to crowd our political and socioeconomic landscape.

There is a dichotomy at play in our community: two seemingly opposing mind-sets debate what is needed to secure a future of prosperity and success for the black community. One mind-set is represented by leaders such as scholar, author, and cultural critic Michael Eric Dyson; the other by iconic entertainer and champion of education Bill Cosby.

The argument, terribly oversimplified, can be boiled down to the question of who should take responsibility for the quality of our lives, the individual or the society? When a member of the press asked me whose position I supported, Dyson's or Cosby's, I asked in response that he take a quarter out of his pocket and examine it. I then asked him which side was the correct side. It was my way of saying that both men's views are valid and significant. They represent opposite sides of the same coin.

The problem in my view cannot be resolved by taking sides. We can't separate one side from the other anyway, and won't help ourselves by arguing over who's right and who's wrong. Our well-being is the responsibility of both the personal and the collective—be it society, the corporation, the government, or community. Everyone has a part to play, a position to assume in order to repair systems that often unjustly exclude groups of people.

This doesn't mean that we must all utilize the same approach. One problem can be approached from many different perspectives. Sadly, too often we spend more time fighting about methods than taking action. A multifaceted approach is often needed for a complicated problem. We must reinforce personal responsibility while challenging systemwide injustices. If not, we will gain the benefit of increased educational opportunities and then realize that the generation we fought for isn't interested in the opportunity we fought to secure for them.

We must lay aside the distracting dialogues of the debate teams and invest ourselves in what we can do, step-by-step and day by day. Our own bickering often assassinates the progress we claim to promote. We must honor the faithful investments of our ancestors with ownership of our abilities and utilization of our capabilities.

Look back at your family photo album. Review the stories you've heard about your grandparents, and their parents. All of them have brought you to this point in time. They were all investing in you and me. If we settle for less than what we're capable of, we are squandering their investment and leaving future generations less than their legacy.

All injustices are not a black-and-white issue.

Persevere to Prevail

To be sure, life itself is not fair. No matter who you are or what circumstances you may find yourself in, it's guaranteed that some aspects of your life will seem to limit you. I have seen families give up their faith after the devastation caused by the reckless cruelty of a drunk driver. Good people develop dreaded diseases; houses burn to the ground, leaving families homeless and distraught. Young men and women get killed on the battlefield, leaving mothers in tears. Corporate downsizing, companies closing, bankruptcy filings, divorces, affairs—all these are equal-opportunity issues that leave us wondering why life seems becomes more difficult for some while others escape untouched. I have encountered millionaires who wrestle to get out of bed in the morning because they feel so utterly depressed. Male, female, young, old, black, or white—each one of us learns at an early age that life doesn't necessarily conform to our wishes. In fact, it rarely goes exactly as we want it to go. Yet we mustn't abdicate the power to make choices that we do have.

You cannot bring back a loved one, but you must not let your grief rob you of loving those who remain in your life. You may not be able to afford the latest-model SUV, but you must not let that prevent you from getting where you need to go. You may not have the capital required to begin your new business full-time, but you must not let that keep you from selling your product to friends and neighbors. You may not be qualified for the new position that just opened up in your company, but you must not let that keep you from enrolling in night courses at a community college. You may not have the partner you long to love and to help parent your children, but you must not let that keep you from investing in your kids' future as much as possible.

I recently invited friends over for dinner. My friend and his sister happen to both practice medicine in the city where I live. They brought their mother, and among the many topics we discussed that evening were the mother's various accomplishments. She had been divorced for many years and raised her five children alone. All five of them went on to do something notable with their lives, in part due to a higher education.

With tears in his eyes, my friend said, "My mother is my hero," while his wife, who was also with him, nodded in agreement. This was a black family paying tribute to their matriarch, knowing that she had beaten the odds.

With relentless tenacity, this now frail little lady beat the odds. Since I now have three of my own children in college, I silently prayed, "Lord, let me beat those odds also." We have far more to work with than she did. But beating the odds isn't always about advantages as much as it is about relentless courage. My wife and I have struggled to give our children a leg up and not a handout. I am not sure what the future holds, but I do know that beating the odds isn't a science. Some turn to the past to strengthen them for a brighter future, and some succumb to the rage and blame, not realizing that *anger without action leaves us bitter and not better*!

Voice your outrage. Say it over and over, write it down and burn it in a bonfire, vent to your best friend, or scream it to your counselor. LIFE ISN'T FAIR. Get it out of your system as much and as regularly as you need to, but do not allow this truth to halt you in your progress forward.

In the prior chapter, we looked at the life of Joseph as an example of how God can turn around even the worst situations. Left for dead by his brothers then sold into slavery, falsely accused of rape by his boss's wife and imprisoned, still Joseph never gave up his dream. He held on to what God had revealed to him and to who God said he was, not succumbing to the circumstance-based temptation to become an embittered victim. Through it all, Joseph clung to God's promises and faithfulness and saw his situation reverse itself by 180 degrees. His ascent from prisoner to prime minister allowed him not only to see his own life redeemed but that of his family as well.

Joseph's maturity, born of suffering, serves as a model for us. To his brothers, he said, "You intended to harm me, but God intended it for good to accomplish what is now being done, the saving of many lives" (Genesis 50:20, NIV). Similarly, you must have faith to know that someday you will be able to say the same thing to your enemies, your persecutors, those who called you a loser, and those who hurt you along the way. What they intended to harm you, deter you, defeat you, God will use to build you up, to heal you, to secure your success.

What is your suffering moving you toward? What is the basis for the passion that fuels your dream? Do you dare to hope that God has the power to transform even the most horrendous events in your life into catalysts for unimaginable success?

Rebound to Rebuild

Not long ago, I went to the Bahamas to address a pastors' conference and work on this book. As I wrote, sitting on the deck of a magnificent resort hotel, I was more than a little distracted by the exquisite beauty of the late afternoon sun. Golden rays cascaded over the translucent blue ocean. White sands and palm trees framed this picture postcard of a tropical Eden. The fresh salt breeze refreshed my senses and my soul.

Just a year before, Hurricane Rita had submerged this very area. The category-five gale-force winds of that storm bludgeoned the place with sheets of rain. Just months before, the site that I now looked out over had been ten feet underwater.

What a terrible experience for the local inhabitants. What could they do in the aftermath of the storm? They could move out or move on. They could let this setback run them out of their homes. Or they could learn from the experience how to be better prepared for the next catastrophe.

The locals reinforced something that I had experienced in the ravaged city of New Orleans after Katrina. As cochair of the Interfaith Advisory Committee for the Clinton-Bush Relief Fund, I met many of the experts called in to rebuild the devastated Gulf Coast. One of the construction engineers told me that in rebuilding the area, new materials, building designs, and the latest technology were being implemented so that future storms would not wreak the same havoc. They were doing all they could to learn from Katrina and turn it into an educational opportunity that would save future lives and prevent future property damage. Like my friends in the Bahamas, the builders in the areas hit by Katrina learned to rebound by rebuilding a stronger foundation.

Lose the Battle to Win the War

Great generals know that they may lose some battles, but they don't worry about this because ultimately they will win the war. They understand that the lost battles provide them with opportunities to better fortify themselves against the enemy later on. They understand the importance of perseverance. My brothers and sisters, you must cling to this truth no matter how sharp the pain of life is. You must dig in deep and never give up.

We must not give up on ourselves or one another and continue using the power of our minds to beat the odds. After raising her family and managing her household, my grandmother went back to college in her forties for a degree in education so that she could fulfill her lifelong dream of teaching. She used the transition period that we now call the empty-nest stage as an opportunity to soar. She successfully completed her degree, taught throughout her fifties, and became a tremendous motivator of the young people who passed through her classroom. When she retired in her midsixties, she had the satisfaction of knowing she had successfully fulfilled her dream and made an impact.

I don't care how old you are, what you've been through, or how many battles you feel like you've lost: it's never too late to win the war. For some of you, repositioning yourself will require you to rekindle the cold ashes of what was once your fiery passion. You will have to allow yourself to hope again and to take small steps toward the goal of becoming who God created you to be. It may include picking up a new trade or skill. It may mean going back to school or helping someone else who is going. You can help a student with a part-time job or give to a scholarship fund. There are many ways to get in the fight! I am simply saying that if you are not moving forward, then you are inching backward. Let's get in gear and make some forward motion with the days and strength we have inside of us!

Surround Sound

One of the best ways we can envision our own success is to have clear role models or personal heroes. Whether it's Lance Armstrong beating cancer to win the Tour de France, Toni Morrison winning the Nobel Prize for literature, or Nelson Mandela overcoming the brutality of racism to become the president of South Africa, you must seek out those individuals who inspire you. We must surround ourselves with people who give us conscious and unconscious examples that where we want to go does in fact exist.

For you see, our environment is just as important as the equipment we use to build our success. Recently I was a guest speaker at the Aspen Institute. While attending one of the sessions at this conference, I was astounded to learn from a panel of highly influential educators that children often succeed even when they are raised in dysfunctional homes as long as they are raised in a good neighborhood. I was shocked. While the members of the panel were not encouraging or condoning dysfunction, they were saying that the community that surrounds children has more influence on them than the house they go home to.

Despite my initial amazement, after I thought about it a while, the idea seemed plausible. According to the institute's Education and Society Program, and its director, Nancy Pelz-Paget, children are more influenced by neighborhood values than by their home life because they spend more of their waking hours outside the home. It does indeed take a village to raise a child. If children are exposed to caring individuals, role models, and examples of healthy people, they can still succeed, no matter how challenging life with their immediate families may have been.

Like the ever-impressionable minds of our children, we are influenced by the people around us. In short, one cannot run with chickens and then soar with eagles! As we saw on the television show *Lifestyles of the Rich and Famous,* winning is more than objects and trophies, artifacts and accomplishment—it's a lifestyle! Real estate appreciates or depreciates based on "comparables" in the community. It isn't enough to build a great house if we do so in a depleted neighborhood. Location is the first rule of real estate—maybe it is for all aspects of living as well. One thing that helps us to develop a fulfilling and encouraging lifestyle is to get around people who are moving in the same direction we are, people who are in our same "neighborhood" regarding their goals and commitment to excellence. These people help to shape our habits, and our habits help to develop our character, and all of these together create the lifestyle of high achievers!

He who gets out of prison only to return to his old environment is setting himself up for incarceration. You must escape the environment and begin anew. Many men with good intentions want to come back and change the neighborhood in which they grew up. But be careful; you cannot change what you are not aware of. Jesus said, save yourselves from this untoward generation. If you're aware of what confines you, then you can overcome it. If you can escape it, you can transform it. But you cannot transform what you are being influenced by unless you face it squarely. How can a bigot transform racism? How can an arrogant manager prevent selfish pride from manifesting itself in the players on the team? You must see what is true about your situation and your giftedness if you are to reposition yourself successfully.

The reason our church started our Texas Offenders Reentry Initiative (TORI) was to help young men and women find their way to a place of rehabilitating their lives by repositioning them. Churches and all community institutions can help facilitate the change people are after, one life at a time. We can give them a new sense of "surround sound" by placing them in a healthier environment. We can bring them new music with which to choreograph the steps of their new lives. We can help them with such basic tasks as filling out applications for jobs and schools and finding places to live as well as offer them a sense of emotional and spiritual support.

Moses was a criminal exiled from Egypt's penal system who found his purpose and became a leader of millions of people. The apostle Paul wrote half of his works—God-inspired epistles from which we still draw wisdom today—from a jail cell. Elijah was an outlaw when God appeared to him in a vision. Each of them had circumstances to overcome and transcend in order to make a major contribution. They would not accept current conditions when they knew they were created for so much more.

As Moses, Paul, and Elijah knew, it is never too late to reposition yourself. One of the reasons my heart breaks for the many men and women I have met in prison is that most of them are highly gifted, intelligent, and creative. How, then, did they end up in prison? And what keeps them from changing once they've been released? In short, one of the contributing factors is often the environment in which they developed. Who would place a green plant in a dark room and expect it to survive, let alone grow? Or what photographer would try to develop a great picture in a sunroom at noon?

Environment has so much to do with results. The sounds that surround you can have an incredible impact on who you become. Therefore, you must find someone who does what you want to do and learn more than the craft itself. Learn the mind-set of champions, the attitude of people who achieve in that field, and assimilate more than information. You will discover yourself developing the lifestyle of a winner simply by associating with those who are what you want to become!

Student of Your Own Success

Another way to level the playing field and beat the odds that may be stacked against you is to become a student of your own success. I know all of us are not wired to go back to school as my grandmother did. Some do not have the support base to do that. However, education isn't always confined to the hallowed halls of esteemed learning institutions. We all must "get in where we fit in" (which, interestingly enough, is an old African-American saying) and achieve education even if we have to inhale our learning from secondhand smoke. This is to say that if you can't go back to school to sharpen your skills, you can read the thoughts of those who do what you do. All universities are not made of stone nor all teachers in front of chalkboards. Life is a school, books are an opportunity to sharpen our minds, and, yes, even magazines feed the flames within the soul. Allow me to explain.

Several years ago I was interviewed by a bright and adept journalist who seemed fascinated at my varied interests and businesses outside of the ministry. She was with the *Wall Street Journal* and was used to interviewing bank presidents and CEOs of Fortune 500 companies. On the other hand, I was accustomed to being interviewed by journalists from religious publications who want to know about my prayer life and how old I was when I knew I was called to ministry. This woman, who was familiar with the characteristics of high achievers, surprised me by asking what magazines I subscribed to and what books I had recently read. I realized that she was trying to get a deeper insight into who I am.

As I listed newspapers and periodicals such as the *Wall Street Journal, Black Enterprise, Architectural Digest,* and *Forbes,* she seemed surprised that my interests far exceeded the garden variety of reading on ministry and counseling. I do not criticize this focus—in fact, I admire it. As a minister, I must remain up to speed on my primary focus. But this doesn't mean that you and I have to be myopic or minimize our interests when they extend beyond the expected.

Incorporating the language and attitude of those who do what you do comes from reading the thoughts of those who think in the vein of your interest. Can you imagine a designer who didn't subscribe to *Interior Designs*? Or can you imagine an architect who didn't subscribe to *Architectural Digest*? Just think of a CEO who never reads the *Wall Street Journal*. Reading is one of the ways of feeding what you believe. In church we would say that faith comes by hearing. What that means is that we believe in what we are exposed to, what is preached and taught from God's Word.

Similarly, we must nourish our hearts, imaginations, and minds with the rich fertilizer of words and images from the fields that we would like to harvest someday. Your dreams may be on a starvation diet if you are not reading articles, gathering stats, surfing the net, or feeding knowledge to your deepest goals and dreams. I should be able to look at your reading habits and see not only what you do but have some glimpse into what you are going to do next.

Root for the Underdog

As we conclude this chapter, I hope you come away with a sense of how important it is for you to acknowledge those areas of your life where you have suffered injustice and defeat. You might even want to make a list of all the events, people, and incidents that you believe have held you back and kept you from achieving more. You may want to discuss your feelings with friends, family members, your pastor, or a qualified counselor. But whatever you do, you must never give in to despair and bitterly resign yourself to less than you were created for. You must take heart and empower yourself with education, exemplary role models, and the latest information about your desired area of interest.

If you refuse to accept defeat of the dream when momentary setbacks alter your plans, then you are well on your way to repositioning yourself for your next stage of success. If you refuse to be handcuffed by the limitations that your environment, upbringing, or peers set for you, then you will discover a limitless source of self-confidence and resilience. Statistics are not operating laws of the universe, locking you in to some unalterable existence. They are simply a brief snapshot of a group at one point in time. They are no more able to predict your future than that freshman-year photo of you in your high school yearbook—you know, the one where you were having a really bad hair day!

Whether it's my adopted city's beloved Dallas Cowboys or the eighty-to-one long shot in the Kentucky Derby, there's a reason that we're inclined to root for the underdog. It's simply human nature. We want to see someone weaker, younger, poorer, or less talented draw on the limitless resources of the heart, soul, and mind to level the playing field and overthrow the stronger, older, richer, or more talented. We know that if they can defeat their

Goliath, then it's possible for us to pick up our slingshot and face our giants.

We are all underdogs, in a sense, for if we accept what life dictates to us, then the statistics can become a self-fulfilling prophecy. But if we dare to rise above and beyond the limitations of our lives, then we grow stronger and wiser, more willing to dream and dream big.

No matter how unfair life seems or how often you may have failed in the past, you can still change and improve your life. And not only change, but grow into the best, most authentic version of yourself that you can be. My friend, it's time to stop feeling that the odds are stacked against you and time to start stacking the odds in your favor!

five
Divine Direction—
Branding Is Better
Than Brooding

When Jesus had finished speaking, he said to Simon, "Put out into deep water, and let down the nets for a catch."

—*Luke 5:3 (NIV)*

When I was a boy, I often ran errands for my mother, including jogging down to the grocery store a few blocks away to remedy our latest depletion of milk, bread, or eggs. I loved going to the place with its parquet floors and push-button cash registers that now seem old-fashioned. One of the things I loved most was the bank of candy and novelty machines filled to the top with brightly colored gumballs in one, peanuts in another, toys in yet another still. Of course, there was one in particular that was my favorite. It held "Super Balls," those hard plastic little spheres that were often clear with a rainbow swirl of red, blue, green, and yellow trapped inside. I would put my hard-earned dime in the slot and turn the handle, eager to bounce my new toy all the way home.

I loved bouncing Super Balls because they seemed to rebound all the way up to and beyond the spot from where I had bounced them to begin with. Although I would not have known the word to use at the time, the one that comes to mind now is *resilient*. Those balls were tough and hard to break—although I think our family dog once managed to chew one up!—and never seemed to lose their ability to spring back as I threw them down on sidewalks and against the side of our house.

Today, when someone tells me they hope to "bounce back," my mind goes to those hard plastic Super Balls from long ago. As we've seen in prior chapters, in order to reposition ourselves toward the life without limits that we all crave, we must not let our past mistakes and painful disappointments prevent us from succeeding. In fact, we must be like those Super Balls that always come back for more, having lost little of their inherent force. Since bouncing back from our mistakes is not just a requirement for repositioning ourselves but a strategy for discovery as well, I want us to examine what it means not only to learn from our less-than-best choices but to transform such errors in judgment into opportunities for coming back stronger the next time.

On the Rebound

Whether it's your favorite sports team, such as the beloved Boston Red Sox, or a talented actress, such as the lovely soap-opera star Susan Lucci, we've all watched as a team or individual repeatedly becomes a finalist but for whatever reason can't seem to win the prize. But neither the team nor the actor gave up. They remained undaunted by their past losses. It took the Red Sox eighty-six years to achieve the World Series title in 2004. Ms. Lucci was nominated eighteen times and came up short each time before winning the Emmy Award in 1999 for Best Actress in a Daytime Drama.

It took Thomas Edison several years to develop a commercially feasible electric lightbulb. It took George Washington Carver a lifetime to develop the dozens of inventions, applications, and products that grew out of his work with the peanut and other agricultural products. It took Dr. Jonas Salk almost ten years to develop the polio vaccine, preventing an illness that at one time claimed the lives of thousands of children and adults in this country.

We could go on and on listing the numerous achievements and contributions made by those who have had to use trial and error, persistence, and an unrelenting vision to reposition themselves from failure. Where would we be now (other than in the dark!) if Edison had decided to quit after his first attempts to harness electricity failed? How many diseases would still be running rampant if doctors such as Jonas Salk had not persisted in the laboratory? It's a fact of life, particularly for those individuals committed to living without limits, that you must live on the rebound.

Like the skyrocketing bounces of a Super Ball, you must rebound higher and farther than the place where you started. You must embrace the fact that failing is part of life, part of your life, and a greater part of a successful person's life. I say a greater part because I believe people committed to fulfilling their true potential are more sensitive to their mistakes than the average person. It seems ironic, but I believe the truly successful are more sensitive in that they pay greater attention and observe more carefully. Interestingly enough, as sensitive as they may be to their losses and botched experiments, they do not take them personally.

This is a crucial point that we must explore for a moment. So often when we attempt a new venture, our initial enthusiasm and the novelty of the activity compel us forward. I'll never forget attempting to learn how to play golf. I had friends who were into it, and they were always talking about putting and driving, handicaps (not physical liabilities, I discovered) and tee times (not a time to drink a hot beverage and nibble a cookie, I also discovered). So I took lessons from the golf pro at one of the best courses in our area. I showed up religiously for my lessons, practiced hitting the ball into the little cup in my office, bought a set of clubs, the shoes, the pants, the golf shirts and sweaters.

But I never really enjoyed golf. I enjoyed so many aspects of it—the social interaction with other men, being outdoors in the green-manicured splendor of God's Creation, and whizzing along in the golf cart. But soon I grew tired of the lessons and dreaded them. I got bored with hitting the little ball in the cup. My tee times were spaced further and further apart until finally I gave myself permission to disengage from this new pastime in which I had invested so much time and resources. I didn't have to keep trying and hope that I would grow to enjoy it more. No matter how long I walked around with that stick in my hand pretending to be Tiger Woods, I was still me, hacking away like a man with a machete in the jungle!

And you know what? It didn't bother me. I could laugh at myself and appreciate the new terms I had learned that would enable me to converse with friends for whom golf is a passion. I had enjoyed some exercise in some of the most beautiful settings around the country. And I had discovered that I was not cut out to be a golfer! It's just not my thang, and that's okay. But the temptation for many of us is either to refuse to quit and continue to torture ourselves, or to end the new venture and feel like a quitter. It's been said that "quitters never prosper"; I disagree. Quitters do prosper if they know that they do not have passion for a given activity and learn from it what they can—about themselves, about others who do enjoy it, about life.

People who persevere to succeed in life pay as much attention to their mistakes as they do to their accomplishments. They learn from their failed attempts and either try harder the next time or readjust their energies toward a more passionate goal. After my flirtation with golf, I discovered that I much prefer lifting weights in order to stay fit. It's an activity that I can enjoy over the long haul and patiently progress in.

What are some of your greatest mistakes in life so far? What have you learned from them? About yourself? About other people? About how to succeed in life? Which describes you more accurately: someone who keeps doing something even if they're not passionately motivated, or someone who quits and feels like they failed? The trick is to find a middle ground between these extremes and to pay attention scrupulously to what can be learned when events and decisions do not turn out for the best. In fact, our greatest learning opportunities often emerge from our greatest failures. Unfortunately, we're often too caught up in our emotions to notice the more objective data emerging from the event. What we may discover is that it's not our poor choices that result in our disappointment. We might discover that we're simply fishing in the wrong spot.

Quitters Can Prosper, Too!

When He had finished speaking, He said to Simon, "Put out into deep water, and let down the nets for a catch." Simon answered, "Master, we've worked hard all night and haven't caught anything. But because You say so, I will let down the nets." When they had done so, they caught such a large number of fish that their nets began to break. So they signaled their partners in the other boat to come and help them, and they came and filled both boats so full that they began to sink.

Luke 5:3–5, (NIV)

Can you relate to Simon Peter's frustration? You've been working hard throughout your entire life—juggling two jobs, taking classes online, rabidly consuming every byte of data about your intended field—only to experience the disappointment of not reeling in the catch you were after. You bait your hooks and cast your nets repeatedly, hoping that this deal will be the one, this relationship will last, this opportunity will finally deliver. Only to face disappointment again and again as your repeated attempts and empty nets leave you exhausted and frustrated.

The above biblical passage is striking to me for several reasons. It's interesting that Jesus tells Peter to "put out into deep water" as if perhaps he has been casting in the shallows. Sometimes it's so easy for us to stay in the safety of shallow water, splashing and casting, wading and wandering around, without ever risking deeper water. We stay in our current position rather than asking for a promotion or applying elsewhere. We resign ourselves to our present relationship even after it's clear to both parties that it's going nowhere. The shallow water feels so much safer—we can both see and touch the bottom of the pool. But this apparent security also imposes limitations and keeps us moored in the safe harbor. Just as in Peter's case, we often have to discover the hard way that the deeper water holds the fish!

Read this passage again and consider how Peter might have felt to have a carpenter-turned-preacher telling him how he should fish. I wonder if he was tempted to say, "Thanks for your input—

much appreciated. But I've been fishing all my life. My father was a fisherman before me, and his father before him. I think I know how to fish and where I should cast my nets." It would be like a construction worker stopping me during a church service and saying, "I think you'd be more effective if you'd move out of the pulpit and preach back there from the choir loft"!

Can you relate to this experience? Have you known those moments when, for example, the new receptionist comes back to you with your memo corrected and rewritten? Or perhaps it's the new sales associate, fresh out of college and with the boundless enthusiasm of a puppy, who asks if he can present a product in a new way. Sometimes it may be an older person offering advice, even though he approaches you with the perspective of someone from a professional field other than your own. All of us have experienced these moments when someone who knows next to nothing about what we're doing and how we're doing it breezes in and provides us with their commentary and unsolicited suggestions.

The temptation is to respond as the expert we are, as the man who's a third-generation fisherman, as the woman who's been cooking since she could stand next to her mother and grandmother and pour in the sugar. But despite this very natural and human tendency to protect our turf and defend our expertise, notice how Peter responds to the Lord. "Master, we've worked hard all night and haven't caught anything. But because You say so, I will let down the nets."

There's a humility and respect inherent in his reply. Peter knows enough about who this man is to not dismiss Him out of hand. And perhaps he feels like he has nothing to lose at this point; after all, he's cast the nets all night long only to watch them come up fishless toss after toss. Why not try taking the advice of a well-intentioned passerby?

And, boy, is he rewarded for his obedience! Not only are there fish in the deep waters to which Jesus directs him, there are so many fish that his nets give way! There are so many fish that Peter must signal another boat to come and assist. There are so many fish that not one but two boats become so heavy laden that they are at risk of sinking! There's something in the water that is beyond Peter's imagination. It's like fishing for a goldfish and having Jaws bite your line!

Just imagine: Your efforts have proved futile time after time after time. A casual acquaintance saunters by and suggests a different approach. You politely smile and courteously agree to give it a try, eager to please the kind novice and send him on his way. Only to find that he not only knows where the fish are, but he has directed you to the richest load of fish you've ever seen in your entire life!

So often in our lives and professional development we plateau on a level of competent complacency where nothing we do seems to break us through to the next level. We see promotions given to individuals who have been with the company a shorter time than ourselves. We see our attempts to start our own business sputter and die as investors change their minds, market trends change, and opportunities for retail space pass us by.

But then it can all change in a second when someone points out a subtle way we can adjust our approach. Like a tennis pro adjusting the angle of her racket as she serves or a golf player altering his stance and the angle of his hips, we often discover that the best advice can come from unexpected places.

The key is not to allow our frustration, past disappointment, present complacency, or personal pride to blind us to those opportunities. No matter how new to the company, an outsider often brings a fresh perspective that can innovate tired systems and worn-out procedures. In fact, I would encourage you to seek out the perspective of others, particularly if you are struggling on your journey toward your goals. Certainly the insight of those ahead of you is invaluable, and I cannot emphasize the significance of a generous mentor. However, you must also be on the lookout for the unexpected and unorthodox perspectives of those whom you wouldn't normally be inclined to consider. The result may astound you in its ability to transform your efforts into a ship weighted with success beyond measure!

What's Behind Door Number Three

Whether it's door number one, two, or three, or briefcases positioned with escalating amounts of cash, we've all seen game shows where contestants are presented with numerous options from which they must choose. The process of elimination then begins and they must often decide whether to stick with their first choice or switch to another, presumably more lucrative, selection. Will they find a million dollars or a single dollar bill in their case? Will it be a new Escalade or an old donkey behind door number three?

Perhaps our choices to reposition ourselves in life are not as overtly dramatic as the ones on these game shows. Nonetheless, we are confronted, bombarded even, with choices on a daily basis that contribute to how we find ourselves positioned and repositioned for success. Should you send your résumé to your friend at a rival company or keep it to yourself out of fear that your boss might find out? Should you invest your time in improving your computer skills or work on conflict-resolution training instead?

On and on our options parade before us like horses on a child's merry-go-round, and if we're not careful, we may end up standing and watching them go by instead of riding and reaching for the brass ring. When my oldest daughter was a toddler, my wife and I were at an old-fashioned amusement park, and of course my little girl was drawn right to the enchanting music and brightly colored animals of the carousel. When it came her turn to board, she ran from the pink horse to the blue one to the yellow one, flabbergasted by the next one just a little bit more than the one before. Finally, her indecision was holding up the ride for the other children and the attendant asked her to step off and wait until she could commit to a horse and stay with it. Needless to say, she burst into tears!

It seems like such a vivid example of where we often find ourselves. For you see, the hardest part about making decisions is not choosing between a good opportunity and a dead-end one. It's not choosing between a good opportunity and a great one—if one is clearly better, then what's so hard? No, it's choosing between a good opportunity and another good opportunity. Those are the times when you could see yourself flourishing in both options, and it's killing you to have to choose between them, as much because you don't want to be disappointed by one as that you don't want to wonder "what if?" about the other.

And perhaps the most difficult aspect of choosing among several strong options is realizing that in order to embrace your selection, you not only have to let the others go, but most times you must also let go of other responsibilities that you're already carrying. In our multitask, you-can-do-it-all-so-you-can-have-it-all twenty-first-century mind-set, it's so tempting to add on more and more and more until we don't realize how much the pack on our back weighs.

Like Peter's fishing boat, we end up so weighted down by cargo that we can't even enjoy the fish we've caught. In my experience, type A, highly motivated, and highly talented individuals suffer this most. Because they're capable, they strategically take on more than their share of responsibilities and commitments. In the church this is often manifest when a new member joins the choir, the usher board, the ladies' auxiliary, and the prison ministry team. They race from one rehearsal, meeting, Bible study, or team exercise to another until their calendar is full and their body and soul are exhausted.

If you are to reposition yourself for success, my friend, you must seek out the options that are most conducive to your ultimate goals. But you must also give yourself permission to close doors behind you, to lay down some of the balls that you're juggling each time you pick up a new one, and to say no to good opportunities if they're not advancing you strategically toward the large goals you've established for yourself.

So many people come to me for career advice, especially when they're torn between two career moves, job offers, or appealing opportunities. After discussing their options and the strong pull of each one, I'm often surprised that these gifted, intelligent, driven individuals haven't attended to the ABC's of who they are and what they're about. They haven't determined what their brand is and how to throw off the limitations of having too many potentially positive options.

Brand-New Day

What do the following individuals have in common: Oprah, Russell Simmons, Sean "Diddy" Combs, Dr. Phil, Beyoncé, Martha Stewart, and Tyler Perry? As diverse and unique as each of these individuals is in his or her own way, each has positioned and consistently repositioned themselves into a recognizable brand. When you see Oprah's name attached to something, whether it's her multi-award-winning talk show, her magazines, her satellite-radio program, or a Broadway musical, you know what you're going to get. When you see Tyler Perry's name on a DVD jacket or on the program for a stage production, or when you see him hosting an event, you smile to yourself knowing that he's going to entertain you.

Each of these successful individuals has followed their bliss professionally so that who they are becomes synonymous with what they bring to everything they touch. They are both recognizable and understandable. They have identity and create, and fulfill, expectations in those around them. In my mind, this is what a brand really is all about.

Identity (who you are and what you're all about) +
Expectations (what others associate with your presence
and gifting) = Your Personal Brand (what you consistently
contribute by your presence and gifting)

Now, I'm not saying you have to advertise yourself on a billboard and be on TV or in the pages of *Time* magazine or *Essence*. No, you advertise yourself every day to those around you in how you present, carry, and conduct yourself. Whether you're aware of it and own it or not, you are already forming a brand in the eyes of others because the more time they're around, the more they come to form certain expectations about what you bring.

From my experience, most people act in ways that are consistent across the broad spectrum of their private moments and public behaviors. If they're aggressive and passionate in the boardroom, then I'm not surprised to see their fervor for the Christmas pageant. If they're quiet and reserved at the party, then it's logical that they prefer one-on-one relationships and work at the library. Now, I'm not saying that we can form judgments and stereotype individuals based on just a few impressions. I'm simply saying that the more you get to know someone, the more consistent their personality seems to become in most all arenas of life.

How would you describe your brand? You should be able to identify three key attributes that you offer in any meeting with colleagues and friends, or any virtues that you bring to a relationship or to a social encounter. I like to call these "deliverables" or to use a fishing term: power lures. (I'll never forget going fishing with a friend and discovering something called "super bait"! An artificial bait in bright colors, often neon yellow or pink, with a strong "natural" smell that's supposed to attract fish. It reminded me of caviar made out of Play-Doh, and I couldn't imagine how any fish would find it appetizing. Nevertheless, its over-the-top attributes got the job done, and we won't talk about how many fish I caught compared to my friend!)

Deliverables are not aspects of our personality that we have to contrive or work at producing. No, in most high achievers, they are natural characteristics and produce the outcome of who they are and what they are about. With this in mind, write your personal mission statement. It can be as simple as: I'm T.D. Jakes and I want to educate, empower, and entertain everyone I encounter.

You arrive at the answer to the question "What is your brand?" by answering other questions: What do you want to be about? What is your vision, your purpose, your mission? Are you demonstrating or rather delivering who you really are and what you really care about? Are you trapped in circumstances where you're expected to deliver what is not even in you? So often when we try to be someone we're not, either from the pressure we exert on ourselves or the pressure from our families, spouses, friends, and coworkers, we find ourselves attempting to deliver items that are not authentic to who we are and what we're about. We end up frustrated, depressed, angry, hurting, casting our nets in waters without results.

But when we grow into ourselves, learning from our mistakes, becoming a student of our deliverables, then we relax and enjoy a level of confident authenticity that naturally sheds limitations and embraces positions in which we prosper, not just financially but holistically, as whole persons at peace with ourselves, content to be who we really are.

Once you articulate your mission statement and develop your brand, don't waver. Commit to it and don't settle for a standard that is less. If you are truly going to know peace and fulfillment, you must honor your brand.

PART II

Beyond the Limits
of Mediocrity

INTRODUCTION

I know your deeds, that you are neither cold nor hot. I
wish you were either one or the other! So, because you
are lukewarm—neither hot nor cold—I am about to
spit you out of my mouth.

—*Revelation 3:15–16 (NIV)*

Leaping out of the cold pool, I was ready to warm my bones in
the refreshing whirlpool of the hot Jacuzzi. Preferring to step
into the Jacuzzi when it was not so crowded, I was lucky enough to
find it completely empty. Then I felt why! Instead of the 102-
degree waters that would warm my tired bones, I found a tepid-to-
cool liquid. I was unprepared for it and my body quickly responded!
As I shivered and hightailed it out of the tub and into my warm
towel, I laughed at the discrepancy between my expectations and
the disappointing reality. An attendant, who must have witnessed
my flight, came over to apologize and to inform me that they were

experiencing mechanical difficulties with the Jacuzzi's water heater. Needless to say!

Curiously enough, the experience reminded me of Christ's admonition to the church at Laodicea, which I have placed above as an epigraph to this chapter. Both the verses as well as my chilly surprise reinforce to me the power of one of the greatest obstacles to success: mediocrity. Let me explain.

So often the greatest obstacle to our success is not the giant looming in the middle of the road blocking our way. While daunting and intimidating, these monsters are at least easily identifiable and often can be eradicated with one powerful, strategically placed stone from our arsenal. As we shift from looking at the obstacles of our past to the barriers in our present, we must realize that even though horrendous hindrances may have occurred, they are at least in the past. Although the consequences of our experiences may continue to affect our choices, we no longer have to endure the abuses of childhood or the powerlessness we may have suffered in an early relationship. We are adults with resources and the power to choose how we respond to the circumstances of our lives. We are no longer trapped by the will of others or the power of past events.

So why then do we often continue to struggle, to buckle, and to settle for less than we are capable of attaining? Why do more of us not exercise our ability to turn up the thermostat of the water heater and rise above the tepid? My hunch is that while we're busy being preoccupied with the obvious giants threatening us, the small, quiet enemy is busy infiltrating our defenses. The water may start out warm enough, but then cools so gradually that we forget that a hot tub is not a refrigerator!

Terrorism of Tedium

A much more sobering example comes to mind. I recall a conversation with a good friend about the devastation and life-splitting reverberations of 9/11. My friend, a professor with a keen understanding of economic and social policy in our country, commented on the painful irony that so much of the 1950s and 1960s was lived in fear and apprehension under the shadow of the Cold War. He and I reminisced about being in school and having classroom discussions about bomb shelters and powdered milk as if they were nothing more than another part of our education, like math and recess. But the Cold War melted into a slippery puddle of diplomatic and economic tensions that no longer seem to threaten us with nuclear annihilation or communist occupation.

No, instead we suffered the greatest subversive attack on American soil at the hands of a small band of covert operatives who caught us unaware and momentarily defenseless against their insidious brutality. With their unmitigated assaults on innocent lives and American icons, they managed to transform tools of transportation and industry into arrows of painfully accurate destruction. The terrorists of 9/11 turned our own planes against us as we sat helplessly and watched the Twin Towers fall, our nation temporarily brought to its knees.

My fear is that too often the greatest threats to our personal success operate like terrorists, stealing moments from our day, sabotaging opportunities to our advancement, and transforming our strengths into weapons of mess and destruction. My collective term for this terrorist threat in our daily lives is *mediocrity*. While I'm sure you understand the meaning of this word, I want you to pause and consider it for a moment. A visit with your dictionary or thesaurus will remind you that mediocrity results from accepting the second rate, the average (or below average), that which is middling, ordinary, commonplace, run of the mill, and middle of the road. Rather than striving for excellence, for the extraordinary, the best, the remarkable and first-rate, mediocrity begs you to stay put and resign yourself to the status quo.

The demon of mediocrity whispers in your ear, "You silly woman, you really think he could be interested in you?" Or: "You old fool, there's no way you can go back to school and earn that degree. Quit kidding yourself!" Or: "Your own business? You can't even balance your checkbook!" Mediocrity places the blinders of the mundane on you so that you cannot see beyond the trials of the present moment—the bills, the kids, the laundry, the stress, the illness, the breakup. And if it can keep you preoccupied with its latest dart of potential poison, then it can wear you down to where you accept the poison as the only potion available. You end up feeling like there are no options, no choices, no resources to defend yourself with and use to overcome adversity and achieve victory.

In this second part, I want us to look at ways we can pursue all three of these objectives—defend, overcome, achieve—in our personal war on the terrorism of mediocrity. We'll look at both the "little foxes that spoil the grapes," as my grandma used to paraphrase from the Bible, as well as those perceived giants preventing us from success such as debt, liabilities, and limited resources. Armed with some new insights and the unlimited resources available through God's strength, you will become empowered to defend yourself successfully and to persevere in your movement toward the prize that God has set before you.

six

Shifting Gears and Changing Lanes— Repositioning Yourself for What's Around the Next Corner

And the lord commended the unjust steward, because he had done wisely: for the children of this world are in their generation wiser than the children of light.

—Luke 16:8 (KJV)

Did you know that I was once a truck driver? Believe it or not, I learned to drive an eighteen-wheeler, although not too proficiently, while I was working for Union Carbide years ago. I was asked to drive it around the lot, and although I never graduated to being asked to take many long trips, I did take a few turns on the road. The amazing thing I learned about driving a tractor-trailer is that the driver must be proactive and does his best work when he remembers to look down the road and anticipate changes. When one drives a regular-size vehicle, sudden turns are not a problem, but when you are driving a substantial-size truck with a considerable weight load, you have to consider every turn well in advance.

Truck drivers have to think about shifting down for a sloping road when their vehicle is weighted and changing lanes when approaching a turn, all because one doesn't spin an eighteen-wheeler around quickly. If my little car can turn on a dime, then this big rig required at least a dollar bill! The truck, with its massive burden of freight, has to be repositioned for the next turn long before the turn comes. The best truck drivers are so aware of their present speed and weight load that they can calculate accurately even those unexpected stops, starts, and stalls waiting around the corner of the future.

Truck drivers aren't the only ones cultivating such skills. In the business world, most CEOs spend a considerable amount of time reading charts like fortune-tellers read tea leaves. They try to determine trends so that they can then make responsible decisions. They base their projections on certain information to anticipate what will happen in the marketplace. They live by the rule that being forewarned is being forearmed. You'll recall the example of grocery giants Kroger and A&P. Both began to see their market change, but only one, Kroger, responded proactively by literally changing their entire blueprint for business. They became a chain of one-stop superstores while their competitor remained stuck in the 1950s.

Would the CEOs of A&P have done things differently knowing what they know now? My guess is that, like most of us with twenty-

twenty hindsight, they would have envisioned the future and acted in accordance with it to maximize the health of their company and the success of their particular business.

If I had known in 1994 that I would be leaving West Virginia to start a new life in Dallas, Texas, I would never have bought a brand-new house in my home state. If I had known my future, then I could have saved myself the expense of struggling to maintain two different house payments in two different states for a year, hoping against hope that one house would sell before I ran out of money and lost my new one. Perhaps I should have paid more attention to the soft market in the area from which I moved. But one doesn't always know what is around the corner. Nevertheless, it is important to start repositioning yourself before you start announcing what you think is going to happen next.

Presidential Positioning

As I write this, we are on the verge of a very significant national election. Much talk is being made about who will be the next president and who is likely to be chosen to untangle the international conundrums we find ourselves facing. Though many credible candidates have been slow to state their intentions, any sighted person can see what is going on when such people are busy having dinners, making appointments with influential people, writing op-eds to important newspapers, and schmoozing with wealthy donors. Why? Because any politician worth his salt would not make a sudden decision without spending quite a bit of time shifting gears, changing lanes, and honking horns as he repositions himself for his next turn around the bend.

Recently I read an interesting and intriguing profile of Senator Barack Obama. In it, the charismatic, articulate statesman shares that he is not certain about his intention to pursue a White House tenure. He mentions that he has to consider the toll that such a decision would take on his personal life and his family. He wants to review all the ramifications if he were to run, thinking through the dramatic changes in his life if he were to win or if he were to lose.

It's interesting to note that I heard a similar statement come from the mouth of then governor George W. Bush when he was asked in a room full of clergy if he had intentions of running for president in the 2000 election. This was in 1998 and he was careful not to definitively commit himself to the arduous task of campaigning for the presidency. However, even then I was aware that he wouldn't have been at the luncheon if he hadn't been seriously considering a run for the Oval Office. Therefore, I was not surprised when he announced his decision to run. It wasn't that I understood politics; it was that I understood driving eighteen-wheelers and that one never makes a sudden turn when driving a big machine. Such preparation is an essential prerequisite for anyone who seriously intends to win at anything in life.

In all likelihood, most of you reading this, like myself, will not be the next president, but still there is something we can learn from those who might be. They do not pray to attain the presidency without repositioning themselves as candidates. I wonder how many of you dream about the future to the point of actively changing lanes, shifting gears, and honking horns to set the stage for what you are going to do with the next phase of your life. Like the big rig driver barreling down the highway, you must know that when you are at the light it is too late to make the turn.

Counting the Cost

What can you and I as average citizens and people of ordinary influence and means gather from these illustrations? I'm convinced that we can gain a lot of information from the legacy of these political giants. The verse from the Gospel of Luke which I placed at the beginning of this chapter reflects the truth that too often, we in the church watch others around us succeed, even those whom we may consider unjust, without learning from their strategies. We must overcome the notion that it's "less than Christian" or "worldly" to anticipate the future, formulate an action plan, and reposition ourselves for success. We must be willing to "plan our work and work our plan," as my father used to say.

I remember vividly the intense strategy I employed in going after my first home. My mother and father had taught me that a man is not a man until his name is on a deed. Regardless of whether you agree with this or not, the reality is that the importance of ownership was continually impressed upon me. To this day I feel sad for people who don't attempt to own anything in the prime of their life. A home is a tremendous asset, and it is difficult if not impossible to garner wealth when one doesn't own a home.

So in my pressurized pursuit of my own little homestead, as I strategized to buy the house when my credit was shot and my resources limited, I knew that I had to plan with all the skill of an experienced truck driver navigating the Himalayas. I had to meet the right people and relate to them with the charisma of a gifted politician seeking to occupy the West Wing. In order to reposition myself for the next maneuver, I had to reduce debt like I was an accounting major studying for his CPA exam. It took some time, a lot of talking, and a few bank people might even say I campaigned for the loan, but eventually I got what I was after because I had learned to align myself strategically for the next phase of life.

Too many people have turned themselves over to what appears to be chance, what they see as their lot in life. They have passively turned their lives over to God, government, or whatever it is they worship or idolize. To accept a decree about how you should live your life without being an active participant is like a blind man driving an eighteen-wheeler! God wants you to turn your life over to Him, but *actively*, not passively.

My rather dramatic comparison calls to mind another situation of throwing off old limits. Recall the incident where Jesus encounters the lame man beside the healing waters of Bethesda (John 5:5–15). Infirm for thirty-eight years, the man asks Jesus to help him get to the waters for healing. But strangely enough, instead of helping him to the waters or simply healing him immediately, Jesus asks the afflicted man, "Wilt thou be made whole?" (John 5:6, KJV). Imagine if you were paralyzed from the waist down and your doctor asked you, "Do you really want to walk again?" Jesus is clearly not being flippant or insulting this man. He's basically asking the man to consider the cost of getting well.

In other words, He says it's up to you. You must stop procrastinating, waiting for others to lead you to where only you can go yourself, or blaming the past. So many times it's much easier to embrace the role of victim, of loser, of the one who's not smart enough, not good enough, not educated enough, not financially sound enough. When you accept such limitations for yourself, then you don't have to worry about being disappointed. It doesn't hurt to fall off the floor!

Instead, you have to be what I call a make-it-happen person. These are the people who see what is coming and they make it happen rather than hope it happens or react to what happens. The difference lies in where you perceive the steering column to be located. Some teach that it is in heaven. Some teach that it is in the White House. But the Bible teaches that it is in you. "Now unto him that is able to do exceeding abundantly above all that we ask or think, according to the power that worketh in us" (Ephesians 3:20, KJV). This Scripture clearly teaches that it is according to the power that works *in you*.

Do you really want to change? Are you willing and ready to give up the past perceptions and perilous patterns that have kept you in the ditch instead of trucking down the highway? Wilt thou be made whole?

Attitude of an Ant

What is working in you that will determine how you handle the next turn? What step did you pursue today in preparation for a much larger stride years from now? It is clear when we look at the illustrious, admirable career of Tiger Woods, with his many accomplishments, prize purses, and trophies, that he has become an international icon. Transforming the PGA, he has wielded his nine club like a sword to vanquish any who don't recognize that he is a force to be reckoned with.

It is easy to see that he is gifted and talented; however, the problem with such terms is that they obscure the fact that he is also a disciplined and strategic planner. He didn't wait until he was thirty to decide that he might take a few golf lessons. I took a few lessons at that age and my clubs are now collecting dust somewhere in my attic. But Tiger started when he was three years old! Imagine how good you would be at anything you started practicing at three years old.

In my line of work, change doesn't come easy. If you think

about the faith world and how long it took the Southern Baptist denomination to apologize for its support of slavery, you can see that the wheels on the church's bus don't turn easily. It wasn't until June of 1995, over 130 years after the Emancipation Proclamation, that the Southern Baptist Convention voted to pass a resolution "renouncing its racist roots and apologizing for its past defense of slavery" (*The Christian Century,* July 5, 1995, at http://www.findarticles.com/p/articles/mi_m1058/is_n21_v112/a i_17 332136). Or consider how long it took the Catholic Church to apologize to the Jewish people for its silence during the Holocaust. In March 1998—more than fifty years after the end of World War II—the Vatican issued a fourteen-page document apologizing for its lack of comment during the Holocaust (http://www.pbs.org/newshour/bb/religion/jan-june98/vatican_48.html). To this day, I know Pentecostals who argue about the appropriateness of women wearing slacks to church. All of this points to how the clutch of the church is often stuck in an antiquated gear of traditionalism.

Now, if the church is headed by men who pride themselves on being bullheaded, then inevitably the people inside the church are taught a slothful myth regarding change and personal responsibility. Leaders who should demonstrate exemplary behavior too often provide negative examples when it comes to anticipating the realities of the future and positioning themselves accordingly. For as we know—and I can't repeat it often enough—the only certain thing about life is change. Seasons change. Children change. Weather changes. Relationships change. Beauty changes. Finances change. Health changes. Strength changes. Every person in this world is powerless to stop change.

Therefore, we must realize that stopping change is futile. But planning for change is not futile. It's prudent, practical, and the golden key to throwing off the limits of your past failures and re-

positioning yourself into the sweet spot of success. We must anticipate change if we are to transcend the futility of repeating the
stultifying patterns of our past. To deny the realities of change in
our lives is to pretend that the forces of gravity won't pull the ripe
apple from the tree.

The young must anticipate getting old. It is foolish for the
young person not to think he or she will ever need retirement
funds. The aged must anticipate dying. It's foolish for the aged and
infirm to allow death to take them by surprise. The single must
anticipate the possibility of being part of a couple one day. The
married must realize that they could end up alone again. A pastor
must think in terms of his successor. He must know that he is
building a place that someone else will one day take over.

The children with their baby bonnets will soon be driving cars.
The Cub Scout troop will disband and the boys will end up recon-
vening at the country club and barbershops. Daughters and debu-
tantes will grow into mothers and members of a ladies' auxiliary at
a church. The members of churches and country clubs will move
on to nursing homes, and the nursing home will funnel them out
into the mortuary, and change will never stop happening.

Even if we accept and understand the realities of change, we
must utilize this information to its maximum effectiveness in the
way we position ourselves moving forward. Some of us just watch
change happen and others of us get ahead of the game and anticipate it happening. As the world turns, the people who get the
most out of life are like the CEOs I mentioned earlier. They track
the trends, they examine the projections, and they anticipate even-
tualities. These forward-thinking people are great at life because
they anticipate the next move and do everything within their
power to make the change work to their advantage. They are not
caught off guard or surprised, because they have looked ahead

and already glimpsed the bend in the road. They start downshifting the big rig well in advance to avoid jackknifing into a major life crisis.

They are like the ant that Solomon told us to watch that anticipates winter and during summer builds a fortress against the snow. The ant's instinctive knowledge that sunshine is a changing resource and seasons pass makes it know what it must do to endure the cold harsh winter. Instinctively, it acts in accordance with seasonal changes as an inevitable reality of life.

What would it take for you to have the attitude of an ant? In your line of work, what do you anticipate in the next ten years and how are you shifting and changing lanes in anticipation of that next era? This is what separates upper-level management from the lower levels. Upper-level people anticipate change. When I hire people, I like to hire those who anticipate problems, not those who run from them or have a Pollyanna "it's all in God's hands" approach to life. You can't lead in life and be a Pollyanna. You must be practical and pragmatic and know that what you have now, whether triumph or tragedy, can't last. In so doing, you can ensure that the next stage is as comfortable, or as lucrative, as possible. Do not allow it to take you by surprise.

Heretic to Healer

Another recent example of a successful corporation anticipating the future and acting accordingly comes to mind. I read that Fox has opened up a faith division to produce films involving family values and a Judeo-Christian worldview. This occurred after they saw the success of *The Passion of the Christ* and *Woman, Thou Art Loosed!* and other faith-inspired works that had touched a niche market that had not been a part of their previous projections and plans. But once they got the point, they quickly began to prepare to be a part of this trend. Sadly enough, churches often spend their energies trying to stop a change rather than preparing for it.

Today, companies are seriously looking at world and market changes outside of their normal range of vision. More and more, they hire people who have the rapidity of thought to adapt readily and radically to new developments in their marketplace. If churches did this, too, instead of fighting change, we'd be further along. We fight things we could learn from, locking our potential for growth and relevance inside an ivory-towered idealism.

I was only a little boy when we started clapping our hands in church to new soul-lifting rhythms and heart-stirring solos. It set the religious community on edge when black churches, where only spirituals had been sung, began worshipping with gospel music. Used to hymns and traditional music, some churches forbade it altogether, and other ministers preached against it feverishly. But in spite of all the clamor, pioneers such as Mahalia Jackson and Clara Ward kept on singing. Eventually, that trend overtook the traditions. A change was imminent. Today, no one bats an eye at what we call traditional gospel music, forgetting the fact that what is traditional now was controversial only a few years ago. The new controversial religious music sounds stylistically like hip-hop and R&B, even rock. Tomorrow, prevailing attitudes in the church toward that music may open up as well.

Innovation is often the catalyst for change at the expense of tradition. Anyone with a sense of history can tell you that many of the organizations that now embrace and revere Dr. Martin Luther King Jr. once actually hated him, resented him, and would not allow him to speak before their members. Long before King's birthday was declared a holiday by our government, he was labeled a communist and enough of a threat to national security for his hotel rooms to be wiretapped. He was feared and resented by many individuals and organizations, even among the black religious community.

There were rumors of him not being allowed to speak on the day he made the "I have a dream" speech. It's ironic that he is now so revered by the mainstream as a significant player in American history. King embraced change, he looked ahead and anticipated that the struggle did not end with the success of the civil rights movement; it could be expanded to address worldwide issues as well. He was a true innovator.

If you and I can muster the courage to withstand the controversy and the same kind of brutal attacks that were inflicted upon him, then you will realize that today's heretic is tomorrow's healer.

I am warning you about the inevitable traffic on the road to greatness. You will not change lanes easily or without a few expletives and hand gestures thrown your way, since your ascent may inconvenience those whose commitment to tradition defies logic and undermines progress. Do not be surprised when they hurl their insults at you. They are out of step. Rightly or wrongly, they will point to the fact that you have driven your truck into their lane, as you position yourself for what will happen next.

My counsel to you is to make sure your mirror is set so that you can see the past without allowing it to distract you from the present. Learn to interpret the road signs and traffic patterns and respond according to your own course and destination, not someone else's. Don't be afraid to blaze your own trail when necessary, knowing that you are very likely paving the way for the success of others behind you. Keep your peripheral view clear enough so that you see who and what may be approaching from the sides. And as we used to say in West Virginia, put your pedal to the metal, good buddy, and lay the hammer down! All things are possible to you if you believe, conceive, and receive.

seven

Ready, Aim, Fire— Launching Yourself Toward Your Highest Goals

Aim for perfection, listen to my appeal, be of one mind, live in peace. And the God of love and peace will be with you.

—*2 Corinthians 13:11 (NIV)*

Several years ago a friend and I had some time to kill and he decided to take me to a firing range. This was quite unusual for me, as I do not normally go to gun ranges or consider pulling a trigger a favorite pastime. However, I was intrigued by my friend's passion and wanted to investigate this hobby that he found so satisfying.

As we pulled up to the firing range, we hurried inside and paid the fees that would permit us to do the target practice. Once we were downstairs where the targets automatically rotated for each shooter in his individual stall, the only thing you could hear above the gunfire was the consistent command "Ready. Aim. Fire!" It was an exhilarating feeling to see the targets moving closer and closer on the wire rods while we, with our ears plugged and one eye closed, were busy trying to hit the bull's-eye. One thing was quickly apparent: You cannot hit the target if you don't aim the gun!

Arranging Success

Many of us have been asked to hit a target in life, but no one aimed the gun for us or showed us how to hold it. Let's explore the power of repositioning from the perspective of those of us who have not aimed ourselves but have been carried by others. For example, pre-arranged marriages are not the custom in our country. Generally, we marry people we think we already know (but actually we don't really get to know them fully until well after the wedding). And then we spend the next few years trying to figure out how to live with what we got. Most of us marry like kids getting the toy out of the Cracker Jack box. We don't know what we have until we're half-way through the box, and then we have to live with the prize we find, however disappointing the surprise.

But there are cultures that attempt, shall we say, to demystify the process by prearranging a union. The matrimonial systems of many Eastern cultures, as you may know, are based on prearranged and prenegotiated partnerships, typically orchestrated by the parents of the couple. In some extreme cases, the happy couple doesn't even meet until their wedding day—talk about living by faith! To our internet-dating, consumers' mind-set, spending the rest of your life with someone you've never met, someone selected for you by your mother and father, is unfathomable.

Please realize that I am not advocating this method as the way we should be going about getting married. But before we dismiss this concept as quaint and outdated, there is an important point about it that needs to be made. In spite of my reservations about the method, I have to admit that I am intrigued by its effectiveness. It's long been asserted that fewer arranged marriages end in divorce than our usual "for love" marriages, where the partners choose instead of their parents. Many statistical studies and sociologists support this assertion, some claiming that the divorce rate in arranged marriages is less than 10 percent. Quite a difference from the 50-plus percent at which our country's divorce rate continues to hover.

Many experts, including sociologist and author David Myers, point out that divorce is often so stigmatized in cultures that arrange their marriages that it's difficult to make an apples-to-apples comparison. Nevertheless, it seems clear that in many cultures, a union negotiated by parents is more likely to achieve success than the method of choice that we currently use.

While this notion may be surprising, think of how powerful it would be to have trained in advance to be the wife of a politician or diplomat. There is a great deal of difference between what is needed to be the wife of a diplomat and what is needed to be the wife of a police officer. Both are noble professions, but each requires a different skill set and social etiquette. Most of us marry people and then try to adjust to who they are and what they do. Often we have the ability to love the person but find their lifestyle conflicts with our background. We love them but are gradually asphyxiated as we attempt to live in a world for which we have no affinity.

My purpose here is not to digress into a debate about dating techniques but to use this illustration to make a point about the power you ascribe to the life of your dreams.

Place Setting

Under my leadership our ministry made the difficult and costly decision to build a $14 million college preparatory school in the southern part of Dallas. You see, the Dallas independent school district is one of the worst in the country. The average income in Oakcliff is about $20,000 a year. The decision to build our school in Oakcliff wasn't based on this statistic, but on where we wanted to see our community go. We wanted to place children in an environment that prepared them for the result we hoped to achieve. We offer multiple language classes for them at early ages. We offer computer training and college-level preparation in multiple subjects because, like the couples in a prearranged marriage, I find that children do best when we prearrange their success rather than hoping that they eventually stumble onto what they should have been guided to in the first place.

No matter how successful your online dating approach has been, you must ask yourself how much further along you would be if you hadn't spent time on failed "projects." Whether it's dead-end jobs or floundering relationships, how much more effective would it be to have been positioned for success from the start? Perhaps the number of our achievers would increase if we started talking to children and training them to prosper earlier in life.

I learned from parenting my own children that while my wife and I worked on some issues, we didn't always realize we needed to put our children consistently in environments with other children who were being set up to succeed. As a minister, I am called to help people who are hurting and broken, but as a father, I needed to monitor those whom I allowed my children to associate with. That created a conflict between my public and private roles. That is to say, putting my children around beneficial influences often meant that I had to shield them from exposure to influences I considered harmful. I later learned that helping people as a minister at the same time as you're parenting your children can often cause you hurt. What do you do when helping them is hurting you?

I took my family on a business cruise for influential African-American families, and it was there that I recognized the importance of creating a social environment that was conducive to where I wanted to see my children go. I thought I was going to network on the cruise, but I ended up spending more time observing my children. I overheard them talking about college. I noticed them speaking about business and law degrees as opposed to the normal teenage chatter. I realized then that my training was not enough; I needed to use strategic socialization to provide them with an environment that positioned them socially for where I wanted them to go in life.

Delayed Not Denied

Sons are a heritage from the Lord, children a reward from him. Like arrows in the hands of a warrior are sons born in one's youth. Blessed is the man whose quiver is full of them. They will not be put to shame when they contend with their enemies in the gate.

Psalm 127:3–5 (NIV)

Let's consider the power of positioning from another direction, as revealed in this passage. Happy is the man who has his quiver full! The powerful analogy that the psalmist uses associates the potential of children with the power of arrows. The quiver is the place where arrows wait to be used. It is the place of possibility; it is the place where patience comes into play and potentials are galvanized into action. In fact, there are three stages of parenting revealed in this text. One is the state of reservation; the second is the state of retraction; the third is the state of release. I want to examine all three as we discuss this concept of being ready and aimed in the right direction before firing.

The overarching idea is not about children as much as it is about positioning words to harvest the fruit of your labors. You may be an adult and still need to go through these three stages to hit the target in your life, your business, your marriage, or whatever your goal may be. So whether you have children or not, what's important is that you see the power of positioning and repositioning and how it affects your end result.

Reservation is the stage of understanding where you must hold back from the abuse and misuse of your skills and have the patience that is needed to wait on the opportunity to find your highest and best use. In parenting, we have an obligation to do all that we can do to protect our children while they are in our quiver. This is also a way for us to say to them: You are important and we want you reserved for your highest use, for the fulfillment of your authentic potential as you grow into adulthood.

Too often, parents ignore this reservation stage. We live in a world where three-year-olds have tattoos and five-year-old girls are wearing heels and makeup. When nothing is reserved, we damage the end result. There is a time and a place for everything. I have learned that giving children anything prematurely is not a blessing. Some things have to be reserved for you to grow into. Just as sexual relationships are reserved for adults and not meant for children, so many other good things are not good if they are granted prematurely.

Think of the winners who hit the lottery and magically attain success without undergoing a long process. Statistics show that they easily lose what they attained because they didn't grow into it. They simply don't know how to handle it. If you are pretrained, you can handle all the peripheral responsibilities that attach themselves to success. It's one thing to have the money; it's another to have the system in place to manage the money and the maladies that are associated with having it.

When we get things prematurely, when we don't grow into them, life becomes bigger and success crushes us. Now, understand that *delayed* does not mean *denied*, and just because you have to wait for it doesn't mean that it isn't coming. The first word they shout on the firing range is *ready*. Are you ready for what is about to happen? Is your home ready? Do you have a system in place for winning? Often there are systems in place for losing, but little is done to prepare you for winning. Have you ever thought about what achieving your dream would do to your life? Do you have the systems ready? Are you prepared for what the demands will be?

The reserved stage is just God's grace giving you time to prepare for His promise. I am not against prosperity. I am against those who teach people that they can magically come into wealth without struggle, when in reality wealth has to be managed like anything else. And God doesn't just hand out financial blessings simply because you gave an offering. You need more in place than just faith; you need works and a willingness to learn how to manage what you are about to receive.

God may give it to you, but you have to manage it. He says to Joshua: I have given you the land to possess it. This indicates that there is human responsibility involved in attaining and managing what He has decreed to be rightfully yours. The way some write about prosperity is much like spoiling a child. It may feel good when you're getting blessed, but eventually the result is a spoiled brat who whines for things but doesn't have the sense to sustain what has been given. So David says, leave the arrows in the quiver for a while and let them be reserved until they can handle being released.

Retracting Forward

Before we can discuss the powerful release that we all want and enjoy, we must first understand the retracting stage. Like an arrow caught in a bow, most people go backward before they shoot forward. What do you do when you can see the goal but you keep losing ground? How do you manage the frustration of having it in your sights and yet seeing circumstances that thwart the aspirations you hope to realize?

It is normal to retract before release. If you take a common garden hose and temporarily restrict the flow of water by bending it, the force of the water will be all the greater when you straighten it out. In a similar way, those of us who have experienced setbacks in life often release and shoot farther *because of* the setback and not *in spite of* it.

Albert Einstein flunked out of school. Les Brown was evaluated as mentally challenged. Millionaires are born out of bankruptcies. Moses was called to speak but couldn't talk. Sometimes what makes us insecure and vulnerable becomes the fuel we need to be overachievers. The antidote for snakebite is made from the poison, and the thing that made you go backward is the same force that will push you forward. I believe this has so much to do with why people who come to our schools from third-world countries often achieve more than those of us born here, who take education for granted. It's the hunger to succeed that makes them stay up reading while we go out clubbing. They are generally bilingual while some of us fight for the right to use Ebonics or write as if we were text messaging. They often take classes in several different areas of interest rather than choosing a degree based on the fewest credits required. The misery they have seen or experienced is the catalyst of their ambition. Our proclivity is to think that there are crowns without crosses, and that is a direct contradiction to Scripture. In reality, it is the agony that creates the ecstasy of life.

Who can seriously disagree that it was the water hoses of the sixties that shamed the nation into changing its racist policy with Jim Crow? Were not the deaths of four little girls in the bombing of a church in 1963 in Birmingham, Alabama, a precursor for the civil rights amendments? I'm not opposed to marching if necessary today, but I still remember how powerful a march was when it was preceded by the hoses and dogs. Can we deny that the blood of Martin Luther King Jr. affected the outcome of the march? Who can ignore the power of persecution? Certainly not Christians, who can clearly see that salvation was procured only after crucifixion. It was not what Jesus *said* on the cross that redeemed us; it was what He *suffered*.

Without the retraction, the release doesn't have the same impact. Perhaps this principle is more clearly seen in the life of Nelson Mandela, who was locked up for years. The power to become the president of South Africa was born in the jail cells of that same country. From the desperate depths of apartheid, racism, and injustice came the power of Mandela's ascent. I cannot imagine how this great leader was able to forgive and work for the betterment of South Africa, but then again I wasn't in that cell. One thing is certain: his release would have been without impact had it not been for the degradation he suffered.

Another example emerges in the life of author, humanitarian, and Nobel Prize winner Elie Wiesel. With his entire family, he was imprisoned in a Nazi concentration camp during World War II; Wiesel ended up being the only one to survive the horrors of persecution. As unimaginable as the hell he endured must have been, such works as *Night* make it clear that the experience forged a depth of character in him that he himself might never have envisioned. Wiesel's tenacity, resilience, and willingness to reposition himself over and over again allowed him to become a philosopher, teacher, political activist, speaker, and founder of the Elie Wiesel Foundation for Humanity.

The aiming stage is also the retracting stage. It is when the arrow is retracted that it is also aimed. It takes strength and discipline not to release the arrow too soon. You must be patient and maintain the retraction until the time is right and your release can be as strategic as possible. You want to retract until you know the tension in the bow supports the launch so that the arrow reaches the target and penetrates the bull's-eye.

Released by Affliction

If you read through the Psalms, most written by David, you might conclude that it's good to be afflicted. Whether it's Psalm 119 or Psalm 71, you will find a voice expressing fear, outrage, insecurity, and utter reliance on God's power in order to survive.

> When evil men advance against me
>> to devour my flesh,
>>> when my enemies and my foes attack me,
>>> they will stumble and fall.

> Though an army besiege me,
>> my heart will not fear;

though war break out against me,
even then will I be confident.

                              Psalm 27:2–3 (NIV)

I am sure that my aim has been improved by my agony. I am positive that had I not suffered my little afflictions, I would not be so focused today, for my focus comes from my struggle. I call my afflictions light ones and am embarrassed to include them on a page that speaks of the four girls who perished in a Sunday-school classroom. I cannot call my pain affliction in the same breath with which I speak of Nelson Mandela or Elie Wiesel. But no pain, small or great, is wasted when it is used as fuel and the catalyst for directing yourself toward your most powerful release.

If this analogy of bows and arrows remains too abstract for you, then make it as concrete as possible. Go out in a field with a bow and arrow and try to aim the arrow or shoot it without pulling it back. It is impossible. Likewise it is impossible to be propelled without being pulled. Now for the joy of release.

This is the reward of those who have been pulled to the breaking point. These are the victories and achievements of those whose anguish preceded their actualization. This is what made Nelson dance in the streets. This is what compelled Wiesel to write a Nobel Prize–winning body of work that managed to transform his pain into power.

What is your moment of release? When will you vindicate your pain with the power of your release?

With the force of a pent-up need comes the jubilation of freedom. You can never know how free you are until you understand how bound and pent up you once were. All of us who enjoy health do not understand how glorious it is until we have seen someone who lost it and gets it back again. This is the power of release. It is tied up in the stretching and pulling stage of retraction. It is with that force that the student who struggled all through school, laboring to write papers and take tests, graduates. The celebration is as intoxicating as the wedding night of a virgin man who has come through abstinence to consummation, with the freedom of full expression. It is with the impact of a waiting groom that the first generation of my people voted. It is with the impact of a blissful union that women now achieve their dreams in a country where they were once considered property.

What is your story? Have you been pulled back far enough to earn the right to know that you have been positioned to prosper by what you endured? If you feel you have not been positioned correctly, I have good news. It is not too late to go back through the process of reservation (taking the time to meditate on the new goals and ideas, getting around people who do what you do), retraction (go into hibernation a minute and get the skills you need for the dream you have), and then, with the force of a groom who waited, go for the dreams that have eluded you before. This time the union has been prearranged and is not left to chance and happenstance. Repositioning is a second chance to realign what wasn't properly directed the first time.

We began this second part by discussing the devastation of mediocrity. Like termites gnawing away at the beautiful timbers of a historic home, mediocrity will continue to nip and bite at your heels. But if you are willing to reposition yourself by drawing on your quiver of resources, then you will discover a power born of your greatest suffering.

You will discover that by reserving your resources, you gain momentum and a critical mass of energy to be unleashed at the most opportune time. You will realize that by retracting your aim, pulling back and tensing your strength, you can have a much greater trajectory. And finally, you will eradicate the erosion caused by mediocrity with the accuracy and intensity of your release.

Don't accept a mediocre life! Consider the realities of your life that have brought you to where you are presently, utilize them to position and reposition your angle of attack, and then give yourself 110 percent to achieving all that you are capable of completing in your lifetime. In short, ready, aim, fire!

eight

Deal or No Deal— Counting the Cost of What You Pay vs. What You Get

Come, all you who are thirsty,
    come to the waters;
    and you who have no money,
    come, buy and eat!
    Come, buy wine and milk
    without money and without cost.

Why spend money on what is not bread,
    and your labor on what does not satisfy?
    Listen, listen to me, and eat what is good,
    and your soul will delight in the richest of fare.
                    —*Isaiah 55:1–2 (NIV)*

When I was a young minister, struggling to make ends meet, I would longingly eye my friends' new vehicles and wonder if I would ever make, let alone save, enough money to acquire a new car. Once I had been working at the local plant for a while, I realized that my dream was not so far out of reach after all. After work one day, wearing my hard hat and steel-toed boots, I stopped by the local car dealership and it was love at first sight between me and the new Trans Am gracing the showroom floor. Just as I was making mental calculations to see if that beautiful machine was within reach, someone else took it upon himself to answer for me.

"You can't afford that car, son," said an older gentleman with a fake smile. "Let me show you some of our used cars back here behind the garage." I hesitated for a moment, containing my anger and indignation before replying, "I don't think you know what I can and cannot afford. I'm sure another dealer will be interested in my business." And with that I strode confidently out of the building and off the lot.

I returned a few weeks later, driving the new car of my dreams: a brand-new 1979 silver Trans Am, complete with T-tops, infrared dash console, and, of course, that beautiful Firebird image burning across the hood. I had driven to a nearby town the week before and bought it off the showroom floor of a dealership there. Needless to say, my old friend the salesman was speechless!

While such a car was not the most appropriate ride for a young up-and-coming minister, I loved that Trans Am. It represented so much more to me than just luxurious transportation. I had purchased success, had broken through a barrier (one clearly represented by the salesman's assumption), and had expressed my ultrahip, exquisite taste as well, all through that car.

I can remember when I was dating the lovely woman who became my wife: I'd have the T-tops out, the windows down, some Barry White playing on the dual-tone stereo, and the silver paint so clean it sparkled like sterling. I'd drive through Beckley, West Virginia, down to my destination, taking my time so that everyone noticed me, little more than a boy myself at the ripe old age of twenty-three. For the purpose of the dating game, I was hoping I looked more like a "play-a" than a "pray-a"!

In retrospect, I think my future mother-in-law, Mrs. Jamison, allowed her daughter to go out with me despite what I was driving—not because of it. Months later, when Serita and I were married, my cool ride started losing its luster. Once it became the family car, well, I don't need to tell you what a spilled Slurpee and the smell of baby wipes did for that interior.

After a few requisite repairs, I awoke to some harsh realities about my dream car. It was only a car after all. I was still who I was. I still lived where I lived. My family was still who they were.

This beautiful, easily tarnished asset was losing more than gas as I drove it—it was also losing value. One day driving home—shortly before the car was totaled in an accident—I realized that I couldn't invest my notion of success in the car I drove. As much as I wanted it to look like I'd arrived, perhaps in part to spite the salesman, I realized I was only starting out. The truth was that I had begun a much longer road trip, a journey to understand what money can and cannot buy.

Later, when I was laid off and every penny counted, I learned that when dollars become scarce, one cannot carelessly spend on a depreciating asset. The dollars invested were gone with no hope of any accrued equity. Even the Firebird's luster had diminished. I replaced Barry White's rich baritone with Aretha Franklin's electrifying voice singing "The Thrill Is Gone." I was beginning to understand the power of priorities and the wisdom in my mother's words when she said, "Education is expensive! You paid a bigger price than what was on the sticker!"

Money Is the Answer

We've all heard that money can't buy happiness, that it can't buy love, and that you can't measure true wealth. While I believe all of these notions are true, I do know what the Bible says about money, and it may shock you. My guess is that most have heard that the love of money is the root of all evil (1 Timothy 6:10), and certainly greed for and the idolatry of material possessions can easily pollute our motives and corrupt our hearts. However, as we plunge into thinking through the role that money and material means play in how we reposition ourselves for success, I want us to consider, in very practical ways, what money can buy us and what it cannot.

First of all, according to Scripture—and here's what may shock you—money is the answer to everything. Yes, you read that correctly! In Ecclesiastes, an inspired meditation on the meaning of life, the Preacher writes:

> A feast is made for laughter,
> and wine makes life merry,
> but money is the answer for everything.
> Ecclesiastes 10:19 (NIV)

Now, you may be wondering, if the love of money is the root of all evil and so many passages of the Bible warn against being seduced by the power of money, then how can it be the answer for everything? But think about it—the Preacher is not saying that money will make you happy or fulfill you or bring you peace and contentment. He simply says that it's the answer to everything; any "thing" that can be had, money can provide you.

My understanding of this passage is that money answers everything because it provides us with options—it always has and it always will. Money determines how you got here, when you're leaving, and where you live. If you don't have much of it, then you came with someone else, will leave when they leave, and are forced to live in your current domicile with very limited options. You do the best you can with what you got. Or as my grandmother used to say, "I got everything I want because I know what to want!"

Money answers everything because usually the larger the sum of money, the more options become available. The nonrefundable supersaver ticket in economy class includes blackout dates, limiting when you can travel and how you will get to your destination. If you're fortunate, then your knees won't extend too far into the seat in front of you and your elbows won't be too confined to allow you to enjoy the salted peanuts.

If you fly first class, paying the premium price, you get to choose your day and time of flight, whether you will look out the window or stretch alongside the aisle. You will get to choose what you have to eat and drink during the flight, the beef or the chicken, the white wine or the red, the cheesecake or the pudding. You will be given hot towels with which to refresh yourself and asked whether you prefer the *Wall Street Journal* or the *Washington Post*.

Money can't make you happy, nor can its pursuit, or the things you buy with it. But the freedom of movement it provides, the ease and convenience, and the possibilities of positioning do indeed solve most, if not all, of life's physical dilemmas. Having solutions to problems provides security. Having security and options allow you to focus on other matters and enjoy the nonmaterial aspects of your life.

If you're not worried about how you'll pay the bills if you go back to school for another degree, then you assess the decision differently than if you know that you'll have to work while you go to school part-time. Not worrying about what will happen if your car breaks down because you know that you can afford to have it repaired can be a luxury more precious than a chauffeured limo. Not having to run up credit-card debt to purchase the gifts you want to give to your children and loved ones during the holiday season can be the best gift of all.

There's nothing wrong with acknowledging that life is easier and more comfortable if you have the financial resources to grease the wheels of daily life.

However, it's tempting to make the quality of our life conditional upon this fact and to view ourselves as totally without choices or resources if we don't have as much money as we'd like. Too often people are more willing to grumble that life is unfair than to invest in repositioning themselves for more options.

Gratitude? Priceless

The reality is that most of us are not worried about where our next meal will come from or if we'll have a roof over our heads tonight or a bed to sleep in. It may not be what we want to eat and where we want to eat it, but we aren't going to starve or be exposed to the elements. Most of us are fortunate enough to have our basic needs met in ways that keep us physically healthy most of the time.

Why then are we so eager to have the next, the latest, and the one we saw our neighbor enjoying across the street? It doesn't even matter what "it" is! Human nature seems to cause us to always look over the fence and admire the lovely emerald shade of the lawn next door.

There's nothing wrong with having incentive, wanting to enjoy life more, relishing the fruits of your labor. Yet so many people, even when they know intellectually that money can't provide what they long for, still strive to succeed in a way that is measured only by their bank accounts. They aren't enjoying what they have because it's never enough. In Ecclesiastes again, the Preacher observes:

> Whoever loves money never has money enough;
>   whoever loves wealth is never satisfied with his income.
> Ecclesiastes 5:10 (NIV)

From my experiences and observations, the only way to protect yourself from getting trapped in a perpetual cycle of never enough is to always be mindful of what you have.

The Apostle Paul knew that you must always be grateful if you are to remain anchored in the present moment and not regretting the past or living conditionally for the future. He indicated that you must maintain a panoramic view of both the good and the bad, and he said that he had experienced both.

> I am not saying this because I am in need, for I have learned to be content whatever the circumstances. I know what it is to be in need, and I know what it is to have plenty. I have learned the secret of being content in any and every situation, whether well fed or hungry, whether living in plenty or in want. I can do everything through him who gives me strength.
> Philippians 4:11–13 (NIV)

Like Paul, how important it is that we all have a taste of both. He said he knew how to abase and abound, both to have and to experience lack, and to be content in both. I personally have been privileged to stay in the penthouse suite of many of the world's most opulent five-star hotels, but as an evangelist, I have also slept in the back of the church. I know what it is to stay at Grandma's house on a cot on the back porch. I believe I am able to appreciate what I have because I realize that my level of contentment is not dependent on my surroundings.

This can be such a difficult lesson to pass on to others, particularly our children. Most members of a first generation—first to be educated, to own businesses, to have wealth—have a challenging time getting their children to embrace their values. They hear us, but don't fully appreciate the message we're sending them because they haven't experienced what we have. They have not learned firsthand the lessons that poverty can teach. One successful man turned and looked at his wife and said, "We gave our children everything except what made us great." She looked at him and asked, "What's that?" He sighed and replied, "Struggle!"

So often at holiday time I become upset with my children. For me, Thanksgiving and Christmas were incredible times of family closeness and special foods—Grandma's spice cake, Mama's turkey and dressing, Auntie's sweet potatoes, on and on. We'd dress up and eat too much and just enjoy catching up and being together. But because our children have so much all the time, they don't view holidays this way. I'll never forget when I saw my boys, dressed in jeans and T-shirts, come strolling in at Thanksgiving with bags from Burger King. I thought I would have a heart attack, if I didn't give them one first!

This is why I believe it's so important to teach our kids a sense of responsibility, even withholding things from them until they develop the perspective to appreciate what they are being given. Otherwise, gratitude is so much harder to cultivate.

Capital Gains

Gratitude is also one of the greatest antidotes to complacency and mediocrity that I know. If you're aware of what you've been given, then you want to be a steward of these blessings, both to enjoy for yourself but also to bless others with. Being content in all things does not mean that you accept and resign yourself and don't look ahead and strive for so much more. It simply means that you realize that you will not be any happier if the Mercedes is in the driveway instead of the Mercury. You are not a better, more satisfied person if you're serving dinner on china instead of paper plates.

In order to cultivate gratitude and learn to be content with what you have, you must realize what money can't buy. You must learn to identify those items that truly are priceless. Usually, from around the end of the year into January, people are busy trying to calculate how much tax they owe on capital gains, which, as you know, is the amount of taxable income you pay on the profits made from investments such as real estate and stock. But there is a gain that cannot be measured by a calculator. The Bible says that godliness with contentment is great gain (1 Timothy 6:6). Paul, in his letter to the Philippians cited earlier, indicates that he had learned how to be content whether he had a lot or a little. That doesn't mean that the Apostle lacked ambition or drive; it is just that he knew that something was to be gained by both the struggle and the success.

Almost every autobiography I have ever read, whether it was penned by a supermodel or a CEO, starts with sharing the struggle and telling how they learned their values from the struggle. There is a gain that is not taxable by capital gains. The gain of having a family who loves you. The gain that comes from working your way up. The gain of finding beauty in things that cost nothing. The beauty that comes from hearing a child laugh. The beauty that comes from the calming sway of the mighty ocean. These things God throws in for free.

Do you include such free and priceless items in your personal portfolio? The beauty of a friend who couldn't go to bed after the party until you got home safely. Or the beauty that comes from a child singing a solo completely out of tune with two teeth missing and a BIG smile! For such things, there is no price. The majestic leap of the waterfalls plummeting down the cliffs of a tropical island. There's no switch to turn it on or off, but it runs continuously. I saw the polar bears playing happily in Alaska, never once sliding on the ice, but simply diving into the freezing waters, ignoring all of us who watched their antics from the luxury cruise liners. The bears knew that the best of Alaska wasn't on the boat but in the water.

When it comes time to calculate your taxes for the year, instead of approaching it with trepidation and anxiety, consider it a real celebration of thanksgiving. In fact, I know a family who serves a traditional turkey dinner once the W4s and all the other forms have been sent in. They have learned to appreciate the joy of feeling a mother's hand on the forehead of a sick child. The comfort of a father's arm on your shoulder as you stand outside and count the stars. The joy of beating your brothers and sisters at Monopoly. These items cannot be deducted. They are priceless and have nothing to do with shares or profits.

When you add it all up, the best things in life are free. If you have capital gains but are personally and spiritually bankrupt, it means nothing at all. Consider any number of beautiful, successful, wealthy individuals who died in despair and heartache. Marilyn Monroe's untimely death. Princess Diana's tragic accident. Ernest Hemingway's suicide by gunshot.

If some of the limitations in your life are money-related, then before you begin to take practical steps toward eliminating debt and becoming more savvy with your resources, you must conduct an audit on what you have that cannot be purchased or sold. The cost of happiness is less than you think. When was the last time you had some "retail therapy," as I heard some ladies call it, and attempted to buy yourself some momentary feel-good? Better yet, do you know why you buy things to make you happy? What is it you're really longing for? Is it the approval and acceptance of others? To feel attractive, young, and sexy? To compensate for the lack of a husband? To compensate for what you were forced to do without in childhood?

There's nothing wrong with enjoying the fruits of victory in your hard climb up the corporate ladder. But are you really enjoying them if you never stop to appreciate what you have and who you have to share them with? Before we move on to the next chapter and consider how we can go beyond debilitating debt, I encourage you to pause here and take an inventory of your true perceptions about money. Are you getting what you're paying for? Or are you longing for something that is free and beyond a price tag?

nine

Lions, Tigers, and Bears—Defeating the Financial Foes That Limit You

Will not your debtors suddenly arise? Will they
not wake up and make you tremble? Then you will
become their victim.

—Habakkuk 2:7 (NIV)

None of us would like to wander into a forest only to find our-selves stalked by a group of vicious predators. Imagine your horror as you look back over your shoulder and see the impending danger of a group resembling the big five in South Africa! For our purposes, we might reduce five to three and call them lions, tigers, and bears, realizing that these carnivorous beasts are only symbolic of the many influences that attack our finances and leave us hemorrhaging from poor choices that follow us the rest of our lives. Like student loans haunting now adult professionals, such wild animals leave us breathlessly trying to outrun what's breathing down our necks. Or what of those growling medical bills and snarling unpaid revolving charge cards? Are they not enough to make even the most courageous of us hide under our blankets and cry for our mommies to make them go away?

You can open your eyes now. I promise.

This is the chapter that might have made you wince as you turned the page, covering your eyes with your hands as if you were about to see the next grisly murder in a gory horror movie. This is the one where you know you're going to get some strong interventionlike counsel and practical tips that may require some changes in your attitudes, investments, and invoices. This is Manny the Manager's favorite chapter, the one where he gets to remind you of where you may have stumbled and tripped in terms of missed opportunities, squandered possibilities, and remorseful ramifications.

But it's okay. There is no guilt here, only guidance; no shame, only solutions; and no fear, only faith. Learning how to manage and disentangle yourself from the financial limitations that clutter your life can be one of the most liberating feelings you'll ever feel. It's not that you will become rich and never worry about money again. It's simply that you will feel in control because there's not a crisis, secure because there's a strategy, and fulfilled because you're finally facing the facts.

As we've discussed, money and material toys cannot make you happy, provide you with peace and joy, or motivate you to be a better person. You'll recall that money gives us options, choices, and conveniences that help us proceed through life. But whether you fly first class or coach, you're still the same person. Many people who dress in Armani suits and Dolce & Gabbana dresses don't take anyone to the ball. No, they remain the worried little distraught accountants whose lives suddenly don't add up. They're chewing their nails, and working late, trying to juggle the debts, defray the taxes, and hopefully delay the inevitable demise of a person who publicly lives the lifestyle of the rich and famous. But privately Mr. and Mrs. High Life are battling the over-the-edge antics of false profits!

If you don't have a plan and an awareness of where you are financially, then it's very difficult to reposition yourself for where you want to be in other areas of your life. If you hit a wall of fear, shame, and guilt every time your spending habits come up, then it's going to be a challenge when you want to consider taking that trip to the Bahamas you've dreamed about, or enrolling in night school, or taking your children to Disneyland. Your finances are a kind of lifeblood coursing through the body of your identity and purpose. Money does not provide the heart, soul, or vital organs to your life, but it does carry the nutrients, minerals, and fresh oxygen to those parts.

So let's lay aside the fear, the guilt, the shame, and whatever other emotions may be making your hand tremble or your brow sweat as you read this chapter. It's time to take charge of this area of your life. It's time to reposition yourself as a financially responsible, resource-savvy individual with a plan for realizing your dreams.

Off to See the Wizard

By asking you to lay aside your fears in this area, please don't hear me saying that finances aren't scary. So much occurs in our financial lives that can easily terrify us. What if I'm not able to save for my children's college fund? What if I don't have a retirement plan or 401(k) in place? What if I can't see a way out of my credit-card debt? Should I use my nest egg to pay off my credit-card debt? Or even, how am I ever going to pay my bills this month!

You can feel like Dorothy, from one of my childhood favorites, *The Wizard of Oz*, beginning her journey with her unlikely comrades, the Scarecrow and the Tin Man. As they venture through the forest where those truly terrifying flying monkeys will eventually descend, they anticipate encountering beasts who will attempt to eat them for dinner. "Lions, and tigers, and bears, oh my!" becomes their refrain as they voice in song their anxieties over the unknown. However, eventually they do encounter a lion, you'll recall, the Cowardly Lion.

While Dorothy is terrified at first, she soon realizes that the lion before her is even more afraid than she is! I love this scene because it captures so much about how we often live our lives, afraid of things in the dark, worrying about uncertainties, second-guessing about thirdhand possibilities. And then when we actually encounter one of those fears, it turns out to be something that we can easily manage and learn from. Dorothy learns that she's courageous and brave, facing down not only lions but wicked witches and larger-than-life wizards. She learns to face unknowns and move through them, stronger and more equipped for the next encounter.

Her growth reminds me of another hero who traversed an incredible life journey, constantly overcoming fears and obstacles: David, the Shepherd King, whom Scripture describes as "a man after God's own heart" (Acts 13:22). You'll recall that David, anointed by God at an early age, could not come into his kingdom without first killing the giant. Goliath was certainly formidable, so much so that the entire army of Israel feared him and wouldn't take him on. Then along comes this mere shepherd, a teenager, the youngest child of a large family, bringing his brothers their lunch. And he's the one who asks to take on the giant! First he must convince Saul, the present king, that he's not insane in his request. Let's review their exchange:

> David said to Saul, "Let no one lose heart on account of this Philistine; your servant will go and fight him."
>
> Saul replied, "You are not able to go out against this Philistine and fight him; you are only a boy, and he has been a fighting man from his youth."
>
> But David said to Saul, "Your servant has been keeping his father's sheep. When a lion or a bear came and carried off a sheep from the flock, I went after it, struck it and rescued the sheep from its mouth. When it turned on me, I seized it by its hair, struck it and killed it. Your servant has killed both the lion and the bear; this uncircumcised Philistine will be like one of them, because he has defied the armies of the living God. The Lord who delivered me from the paw of the lion and the paw of the bear will deliver me from the hand of this Philistine."
>
> Saul said to David, "Go, and the Lord be with you."
>
> 1 Samuel 17:32–37 (NIV)

David possessed the strength and confidence to square off against the most terrifying foe imaginable because he had defeated the smaller threats along the way. He viewed those past encounters with lions and bears as God's training ground for facing and defeating Goliath. The future king learned to fight for his flock, sheep by sheep, and from that battle he learned how to go into a situation that others might view as insurmountable.

I believe this is how we must learn to reposition ourselves as we examine our financial lives and the role money plays in who we are and what we do. We must be willing to face the daily fears. David couldn't come into the kingdom without killing the giant. For many people, prosperity—and I use that term not to mean mere financial wealth but to encompass the full meaning of what it means to thrive—is an impossibility because they can't seem to kill the giant—that conglomerate of accumulated fear and financial failings—that stands looming between them and their dreams.

I'll never forget a woman I counseled who came to me after finding herself sobbing in her car on the side of the road. Her flat tire had not only sent her small sedan into the ditch, it sent her reeling emotionally. She said to me, "Sitting there in the rain, I realized that I didn't have anyone to call to help me. And I didn't know how I would pay for new tires or repairs. I immediately jumped from there to thinking I will never be loved by anyone the way I long to be loved. I will never be out of debt."

While this kind of jump can be extreme, as even this dear lady recognized, her feelings epitomize what so many of us experience. We feel so overwhelmed by the little things that we can't imagine squaring off against the big things. I've known millionaires who had collection agencies after them for missing consecutive payments on their homes and cars. Why? Because the millionaires didn't want to have to open the bills, calculate their payments, budget their incomes, and send in the checks. But this is not the way to live a balanced life. This is a self-imposed limit that you can and must break through as you proceed to reposition yourself for a better life.

The More the Merrier

Please realize that you are not alone. I have seen businesspeople—affluent types with button-down collars, applying for top-level jobs—who aren't what they seem. For when you run a credit check, which incidentally is becoming a more routine part of the hiring process, you are shocked that little Mr. Button-Down or Ms. Business Suit is over his or her head in debt and has a credit report that looks like it just contracted leprosy!

From white collars to blue collars, there lies a problem. Big spenders overspend and little ones do, too. And God help the shirts and blouses that hide beneath them a trembling heart that has had more than one crying session, appearing to have it together outwardly but inwardly aware that they are in a financial crisis. I mean, just look at the gross national debt in this country. The whole country is struggling to some degree. From the welfare program to the Social Security program, we are hearing a lot of talk about overspending. Companies are downsizing, politicians are raising money as fast as an auctioneer can speak. Each and every one of them is trying to make sure that they are budgeted for the long haul and not the short run.

White and black, Hispanic and Asian-American, we must all learn to help one another stop the poor spending habits that keep us ensnared in debt.

I, as an African-American, am particularly concerned about the spending habits among people of color. There is an epidemic of poor spending choices and even poorer investing habits for African-Americans in this country. According to Target Market News, a national marketing firm that specializes in tracking the spending habits of blacks, we spend more annually on depreciable goods such as cars, clothes, liquor, and personal-care items than other groups. When our nation's economy took a downturn in 2002 after 9/11, blacks proceeded to spend $22.9 billion on clothes, over $11 billion on furniture (often to furnish rented homes), and over $3 billion on electronic appliances and toys. We spent almost $47 billion on cars in 2005, so much that some automakers such as Lincoln have targeted us as a niche market, creating tricked-out SUVs with multiple plasma screens, DVD players, and PlayStations. According to the National Urban League's report "The State of Black America 2004," fewer than 50 percent of black families own their homes, compared to more than 70 percent of whites.

Where have we cut back? Sadly enough, African-Americans bought fewer books from 2000 to 2003. According to a reporter for the *Digital Digest* (based in Detroit, where the population is 80 percent black, as is the reporter): "This shortsighted behavior, motivated by a desire for instant gratification and social acceptance, comes at the expense of our future" (www.amren.com/mtnews/archives/2006/02/black_spending_habits.php). Amen! I heartily agree and believe that we must sound the alarm and wake up from our reckless disregard for our futures.

We are not the only group of people that has to struggle with such statistics and disheartening trends. Any minority group that must overcome biases attempts to compensate. But many factors play into this issue in our community.

It is not a question of a lack of discipline on the part of African-Americans. Often when people have been constantly belittled and ostracized, they so envy their oppressors that they take shortcuts to gratification. A desperate need to be seen as significant causes the wrong choice of easy gratification, rather than the more difficult task of slowly turning around the financial effects of years of oppression and lack of financial training. It is the incessant need to be important that often has us begging for what we need and buying what we want. Our ancestors came to this country with the sign WILL WORK FOR FOOD. It was a sign called slavery. Though that is over now, its consequences linger. Our forefathers couldn't teach their sons, much less their daughters, about money because they never had any.

Millions of advertising dollars have been spent to target the black consumer, but few have been spent to train our people in the principles of wealth building that are needed to sustain the wealth that exists in our growing economy. Yes, growing, soon to be $800 billion of disposable income, according to a recent *USA Today* article.

Training in financial management is best done in the home, but when that home is shattered or the parents are poorly skilled about finances, children learn what they see. And what do the children see? They see bling-bling from the rappers to the preachers. But little is taught about how to get wealth and, more important, how to keep it. If you try to live the lifestyle of the rich and famous without a practical pragmatic plan, if you spend on depreciable and ignore appreciable assets, you will live a pseudo life, a facade.

Bling-bling without economic empowerment is much like a woman having false labor. She has the feeling of travail but the baby isn't ready. It is a trip to an emergency room only to come home empty-handed. Likewise, diamonds and furs don't mean that you are wealthy. They may instead mean that you are broke. I want to teach this until I do not see another Porsche parked in front of an apartment. I am weary of seeing Prada shoes stuffed under a bed in a room that has no closet. St. John dresses and Jack McConnell hats are nice when you have a trust fund, but when you don't, you will later wish you had eaten your hat! Why are Air Force Ones, those elaborate tennis shoes, on the feet of children who have no schoolbooks! And if I preside at another funeral for a minister who has more alligator shoes than the swamp has crocodiles, and yet we have to raise an offering for his widow and children who are left with no life insurance, I think I will just scream!

Our country must do more to help all people who are poor. But neither charitable neighbors nor government programs will eradicate poverty if they are left to do the work alone. Without educating people in a wealth strategy and giving them a mentor who understands their struggle, any amount of charity is like pouring fresh water into a rusty bucket that leaks. Poor financial habits will make whatever your income, large or small, leak out over time.

It's not just for our sakes but the sake of future generations that we must become more responsible and focused. When I was growing up, my grandmother kept her "savings account" in an old coffee can on the top shelf of her cupboard. Leftover grocery money, spare change, and unexpected gifts were all deposited. It accumulated into quite a nest egg when she was ready to purchase a major appliance or new winter coats for her grandchildren. But today we have poured Grandmother's coffee can into a daily latte at the corner Starbucks, another pair of designer shoes, or this week's bottle of wine. And please don't hear me wrong—I am not against any of these items or the concept of splurging a little now and then and rewarding yourself with a nice pick-me-up. However, when we are slowly digging ourselves into deeper debt and, heaven forbid, into bankruptcy because we have no self-control, then something must change.

Dollars and Sense

Too often, I believe, we get caught up in a cycle that's as dangerous as any riptide hiding under the calm swell of an ocean current.

How do we begin moving beyond these dangerous waters into a smoother, calmer sea? I'm glad you asked. In the rest of this chapter, I would like to offer some tips and strategies for ways to slay the lions, tigers, and bears that come our way. In the next chapter, we will examine how to use this knowledge and these building blocks to defeat that giant debt looming over most of us—our mortgage.

If the steps of a good man are ordered by the Lord (and they are), then here are a few simple first steps that will set you into a jog toward the prize. And realize that the prize of good credit is actually the redemption of your name! I don't know if God wants you rich, but He did teach the importance of a good name. That is all good credit is. It is a good name with the business community. Now here are a few simple steps to retrieve, redeem, and restore your good name by repositioning yourself one step at a time.

Look yourself in the mirror and know what you're worth. By this I mean two things. First, you must face yourself and the emotional baggage you have regarding money and look it squarely in the eye. I encourage you to both journal and to discuss with someone who's ahead of you in this area—a friend, a family member, someone from church. Be honest with yourself and be honest with them. Don't lie or put a spin on past mistakes. If you wasted money on clubbing and eating out, then acknowledge it. How will you prevent yourself from repeating the pattern? It's not that you can never go out again; it's simply being smart about it so that you can maintain feeling good about yourself instead of experiencing the highs and lows of the riptide cycle.

Second, I encourage you to put all the facts about your finances in front of you. Consider it a personal audit, not of what you're worth as a person (which is hard to separate from financial worth sometimes, especially in our culture) but what your assets are worth. List all your debts, of any kind. And not just credit cards, car loans, and home mortgages. Do you owe relatives for past loans? Do you have school loans that may not be due because you're still in school or in a grace period? One way to be brutally honest in this area is to get your credit report.

Did you know that you are entitled by law to receive a free copy of your personal credit report every twelve months? It's true. In fact, the big-three credit reporting entities—Experian, Equifax, and TransUnion—have worked together to create a Web site where you can go to request your credit report and credit score. Check it out at www .annualcreditreport.com. There's an explanation of how credit scores work, but generally speaking, of course, the higher the better.

You want to be in that six hundred and up range. That's a sterling reputation that will enable you to make major purchases at the most advantageous interest rates. You want to be on time with your payments. If you've been late or missed payments before, you might want to include a note of explanation in your file, particularly if you suffered an extended illness, injury, or unemployment that affected your ability to pay on time. If errors appear—such as a listing of that department-store account you paid off and closed last year—then contact the store and make sure it gets corrected.

So often people assume all credit is bad and work hard to avoid using it altogether. It's not bad—it's a matter of how you use it. If you're constantly abusing it and going deeper and deeper into the hole with nothing to show for it, then, yes, it can become a straitjacket preventing you from personal and professional mobility. Yet if you use credit wisely, particularly for investments in properties, you can transform it into real wealth. We'll discuss these kinds of home and property investments in the next chapter, but for now try to rethink the way you regard credit in your life.

Accept that this takes time and will not change overnight. Just as embarking on a weight-reduction plan requires a major lifestyle change and not a six-week diet, you must realize that you cannot continue to think about money and finances the same way. Some days you will exercise and it will feel good; other days you must force yourself to show up at the gym. Or to forgive yourself when you don't. You'll be tempted to eat that brownie smothered with Häagen-Dazs vanilla ice cream, but you know what will happen if you do, both physically as well as emotionally. Getting out of debt works the same way. Just as you can't escape the need to eat, you can't escape the reality that money is needed to navigate through each day. So take the time to start out slow.

Save what you can, no matter how small. If you have to get a coffee can and stick a dollar in it every day and go without a soda or coffee at break time, then do so. If you haven't opened a savings account, then shop around at the banks in your area and see which one has the highest interest rate and the lowest minimum balance. Don't forget to inquire about penalties and extra charges for withdrawals or services, such as electronic transfers. If you have a savings account, then consider investing some of your savings in a higher-yield stock or bond. Save toward investing in a property that will bring you the highest possible return.

The key is to get into the habit of saving and to feel good about it. Instead of buying a new lipstick, magazine, or outfit, what if you invested this money in your savings account (whether can, jar, bank drawer, or portfolio) and spent time (not dollars) thinking about one of the goals for which you're saving. Immediate gratification is not gratifying if it costs more in the long run. You have to learn to get below your impulses and temptations and learn to face what is really going on inside. Are you feeling insecure at work and want that designer dress that screams success? Is he ignoring you so you feel like you need new lingerie to keep his attention? Are you compensating for your loneliness by spending on something that will distract you from your pain? You will never learn to save effectively if you aren't willing to know why you spend in the first place.

Pay off more than the minimum credit-card payment, even if it's only one dollar. As you likely know, if you only pay off the minimum balance on your credit cards, you will end up paying more than twice as much as what you originally charged. Is that new iPod really worth five times its purchase price stretched out over ten years? I say that you should pay at least one dollar more than the minimum just to get you in the habit. If you can pay ten dollars more, pay it. A hundred. Can you pay it off, even if it hurts this month? It's your life you're bartering away here, so think twice about what it is you're really signing on for.

Be realistic about how to pay off credit-card and other personal debts. There are different systems offered by many different experts. Suzy Orman, who has spoken and led financial seminars at MegaFest events for me, has written numerous books on how to get out of debt and get ahead. She encourages consumers to prioritize their debts and begin paying off the debts that have the highest interest rate first until they're paid off. Then use the money that used to go to that debt and apply it to the next highest rate.

Other experts offer a variation with a different motivational tool. Financial guru Dave Ramsey encourages you to pay off your smallest debt first because the satisfaction of attaining it will feel good and encourage you to keep going with the next highest, so basically you're working your way up. He calls it the snowball method and assumes that your financial self-esteem will grow as you wipe out what you owe.

There is no one-size-fits-all methodology here. I encourage you to do some research—online, at your library, and in the bookstore—and see what seems doable—no, *really* doable, for you and your lifestyle.

Look for areas where you can cut back without cutting out what they provide you. One way to help yourself re-envision your spending habits into savings habits is to learn how to give yourself what it is you long for without spending so much to do it. We may never fully separate our emotions from how we relate to money any more than we separate our feelings from our beliefs about sex or politics. But we can learn how to manage them. We can learn when we're spending for the wrong reasons, which only compounds the problem because it does not address the real need. Look for creative ways to honor the need without having to feed it financially.

Do you need to get away? Instead of a week at the beach, maybe you can create a vacation at home, seeing local sites, eating out a few times, and finding silly activities for your family. Maybe you plan ahead for Christmas presents so that you don't have the large expenditures and credit-card-bill hangover in January. Perhaps you can allow yourself to have a cup of coffee in a quiet café instead of the five-dollar flavored espresso drink at Starbucks. You crave the break from your day more than the latte, so why pay for more than you need? In fact, maybe a walk in the nearby park would perk you up more than a jolt of caffeine. If you're willing to get in touch with your true needs, then it will be much easier to know if you really need to spend money on something.

Find an emotional outlet when you are tempted, afraid, overwhelmed, or ashamed. Because our emotions play such an integral part in how we relate to money and how we spend it, we often need a safe place to deal with our feelings. Part of repositioning your finances should involve finding someone you can turn to when the urge to splurge hits full force. Just as a recovering addict has a sponsor, someone who has been sober and successfully in recovery for a long period, you need someone who can ask the hard questions and provide some strong feedback.

It's not that you need someone to police you and make you feel bad when you blow it. In fact, I encourage you not to choose someone who will add to your natural guilt, shame, fear, and insecurity. Instead find an encourager, a person who knows what it means to struggle with your issues and is a little farther down the road than you. Perhaps you can even set up a regular time together to discuss and assess your progress. This person works the way a personal accountant works for wealthy people; he keeps you on task. Such people may not have all the facts about your finances, but they nudge you when you are about to buy that buy-one/get-one-free fur coat. They are the ones who say, "How much are you going to use that mink living in Phoenix!" Or, "Don't you already have that same color bag in a clutch style?"

Plan for the unexpected. So often what gets us into trouble is being unprepared when the transmission on the car goes, when the computer hard drive crashes, when the gas bill triples for the month. If you're living hand to mouth, the tendency is to either get a cash advance on your credit card, which is a terrible idea because usually the interest is not only higher on that amount but it may trigger a raise on the interest for purchases as well, or to borrow from some other source. Asking for a loan from a friend, parent, or coworker is occasionally a necessity, but it should be a very last resort. Too often these kinds of interpersonal loans only complicate the relationship and can cause fractures that may lead to earthquakes of emotion down the line.

How much better you will feel if you have a little bit tucked away for such an emergency. You'll feel good because you don't have to worry about how to pay for the emergency, and you'll feel even better because you planned ahead. You're not off track and upset. Your focus and position have remained true to your goals and the success for which you're heading.

Think in terms of abundance, not deprivation. This accompanies the other strategies, as you can see, particularly in how you learn to view your finances and manage the swirl of emotions you may experience around your relationship with money. This particular strategy—abundance, not deprivation—runs counter to our culture and the role that advertising and the media play in our lives. You see, the goal of advertising a product is to convince you—emotionally and rationally—that you will be better with this product than without it. Hungry? Look at this juicy hamburger or that lobster dinner. Lonely? Look at the good time those people are having at that restaurant or club. Nervous? Insecure? Afraid? Feeling unattractive? On and on rolls the litany of emotional hot buttons.

But if you get into the attitude of gratitude and remind yourself daily of what you have, not what you don't have, then you will discover a freedom from the tentacles of consumer advertising. You will remember that the new necklace won't make you any prettier. You will know that the way to overcome your loneliness isn't to eat out more often. The way to feel better about your skills and talents is not to buy the new briefcase or BMW. You can make more informed purchases because you will be aware of what you already have. You don't have to try to compensate for what you don't have.

We'll continue to think through the obstacles, particularly the giant of your mortgage, and how to overcome them in our next chapter. There we'll look at retirement planning, mortgage options, and building wealth through the gifts of others. But I encourage you to pause for a moment here and think through the emotions that you have regarding your present financial position. Are you where you want to be? Are you even headed in the direction of where you'd like to be a year from now?

As much as it might be enjoyable to imagine, the chances of your winning the lottery or inheriting a million dollars from Great-Aunt Mathilda are slim. But you know what—even if you did have a windfall, the way you feel about money and the habits that are already in place would not change. Repositioning is not about making more money. It is about budgeting what you have and having a plan that considers tomorrow! Even rich people don't always get the help they need to keep it together. I wish you could talk to guys like MC Hammer, who share great wisdom about how easily it can all get away from you. It can happen to anyone—to me, to you, to anyone. I guess that is why we all relate to Whitney Houston when she belts out those words, "Didn't we almost have it all?"

The time is right for you to get it back, my friend, for you to intervene on your own behalf and set a course that will allow you to prosper on all levels, not just in your bank account. If you've already got a plan, then review it and see where it can be tightened and improved. Ask yourself if it's working for you and if it's allowing you the options necessary for where you want to head. If you don't have a plan, or a plan that's working, then I encourage you to begin today. Right now. It's that urgent. If I told you that you would develop cancer if you didn't go to the doctor and get medicine today, I know you would. Unfortunately, debt and financial mistakes can grow and spread like a cancer until they threaten to destroy our foundation and undermine our dreams. Don't let that happen. You are stronger and better than that! Manny the Manager knows it and I know it, too!

I leave you with this simple prayer before we go deeper into what it takes to get you financially into the land of Oz and away from the little Munchkins who are eating up your plans.

Dear Lord, You gave us a planet that is still here after thousands and perhaps millions of years. Please teach me how to hold on to what You have given me. Restore my finances like You redeemed my life. Give me the strategy I need to reposition myself while I have a chance to be more, see more, and enjoy more of life by listening to this advice and applying it to my life. I know You are a God who gives second and third chances. I want one now to begin to reclaim what I am allowing bad information and poor spending habits to steal from me. Thanks for being my accountability partner as my new life begins! Amen.

ten

Facing the Giant— Capitalizing on Credit for Consistent Growth

---

So David triumphed over the Philistine with a sling and a stone; without a sword in his hand he struck down the Philistine and killed him. David ran and stood over him. He took hold of the Philistine's sword and drew it from the scabbard. After he killed him, he cut off his head with the sword.

—*1 Samuel 17:50–51 (NIV)*

Like David, most of us have faced the giant before, that oversize accumulation of debt that seems to snowball into an avalanche threatening to suffocate us beneath the blizzard of bills. In fact, many of us look the debt giant in the eye on a regular basis—at least once a month. From a distance, he doesn't look terrifying. On the contrary, he smiles at us with a wink and a nod and showcases what's just over his shoulder like Vanna White on *Wheel of Fortune*. Whether it's the home of our dreams or a reliable car to get us to and from work, the new boat and trailer for those weekends at the lake or that tropical vacation of a lifetime, the debt giant stands as the gatekeeper to all the material goods and accoutrements that we long for in our hearts. He knows what we're after better than we ourselves know it in many instances.

As we explored in the prior chapter, these material possessions tend to play on our emotions in deep and profound ways, becoming symbols of our self-worth, self-image, and self-confidence. The debt giant knows the power that we've infused into that brick home in the gated community, that Lexus sedan, that tennis bracelet with more sparkle than a starry night. Yes, he knows it and seems to relish the power he has over us because of our relationship to these objects.

And let me make it clear before we delve deeper into exploring this giant and how to overcome him; such homes, cars, and possessions are not bad things. It's not a bad thing to want to live in a new home in a secure and beautiful neighborhood. You're not a selfish person solely because you would like to have a luxurious, late-model sports car or a vintage Cartier watch. No, my friend, the problem sets in when you place more value on such an item than it's worth.

When you are willing to indenture your energy, your time, and your money in order to have something that you hope will bring you qualities that cannot be bought to start with—peace, contentment, love—then you're basically making a deal with the devil. No, I am not saying that going into debt is unbiblical or demonic. In fact, as we will see in a moment, there are incredibly constructive ways to utilize your credit to build wealth for the future and establish your buying power. I simply mean that when you trade years of your life and thousands of dollars of your income for items incapable of satisfying your soul, then you have a major problem.

And the irony is this: Your enjoyment of those items is usually offset by the worry, fear, and anxiety that lingers around them like the smell of fish gone bad in the fridge. You and I both know those gut punches that come when you open the monthly envelope and see the total amount to which the charge card has ballooned. Or you have the new tires to purchase that suddenly makes it a creative challenge to pay the mortgage before the fifteenth. Or suddenly you realize that the amount of money you're paying to keep the boat docked is greater than the time you're spending to enjoy it. There is a huge, intangible cost to the items that we purchase, particularly when we buy them on credit.

In fact, this is how the debt giant grows in both size and power. As our debt continues to snowball, we've soon created an avalanche that towers so much taller than Frosty the Snowman that it's not funny! Whether it's rent-to-own appliances, no-down-payment financing, interest-only loans, or deferred payments, the giant knows how to feed himself, and what he eats comes both from our desires to have more and from our fears about how to pay. If he can make it seem easier, smarter, quicker to us, then he grows another foot or more.

Soon he is looming over us like a slave master—and I do not use that comparison lightly, knowing the terrors that some of our grandparents and great-grandparents faced—requiring more and more from us, squeezing the life energy out of us from every side. We wake up in the middle of the night, worrying about how to juggle payments and borrow money to pay minimum payments on items already consumed or discarded. It's more than crazy when we step back and examine what we're doing! But like an addict craving secrecy because of the shame of her addiction, we keep our business to ourselves, refusing to bring our financial struggles into the light of day where others can help us.

And this is the reality we must face: We often cannot reposition ourselves because we are paralyzed by the debt giant, paralyzed financially because we have not assumed the responsibility necessary to free ourselves, paralyzed emotionally because we live in a shroud of fear and anxiety. It's not that we need or even want to be rich. It's simply a matter of being in control of our resources, our opportunities, and our emotions.

Quality Control

You might be tempted to ask me why I think I'm qualified to address this topic. After all, I am not an accountant; I'm a minister. While this is true, please let me remind you of two other pieces of vital information. I know what it means to face the debt giant and, like David squaring off against Goliath, to stand victorious with the brute's severed head in my hand.

I have lived in desperate fear that my only transportation to and from my job would be repossessed by the lender. I have seen that fear realized as I stood in the driveway, with tears of indignation and anger held back like floodwaters within a dam, and watched a stranger coldly ignore my pleas and drive away with my car. I have watched my wife transform a can of pork and beans into a casserole fit for a king with a few leftovers and condiments, all to feed a family of five.

So I know this giant and his power intimately, and having defeated him, I know his weaknesses, vulnerabilities, and secret Achilles' heel that can precipitate his downfall. I'm eager to share these "fault lines" with you so that you can overcome the power he holds in your life, so that you can pry his fingers loose from the neck of your fragile finances once and for all. I want you to experience the exhilarating freedom that comes from looking over your shoulder and seeing the debt giant lying lifeless behind you. Better yet, I want you to be able to see the path before you clearly, uncluttered by creditors and unfettered by your own fears.

The second qualification I bring to our exploration of defeating the debt giant involves my many years as an entrepreneur and businessman. The Lord clearly called me to be a pastor, often in spite of myself! But he also gifted me with the desire, drive, and determination to analyze opportunities and invest in them. Beginning with a check for eight dollars that I received as a boy from Mrs. Minerva Coles, a neighbor back in West Virginia, for mowing—or should I say scalping—her yard, I have learned how to value hard work and appreciate a dollar earned. I have delivered newspapers, sold fresh fish from the back of my father's red pickup truck, dug ditches, and worked the night shift at a Union Carbide plant.

Through these difficult yet transforming jobs, God taught me so much about attitude, gratitude, and aptitude. Even as I learned that I didn't want to spend my life lifting a shovel to dig a trench, I also learned what it meant to use present labor as a means to future fulfillment. Discipline and budgeting, timing and cost efficiency—I received all my lessons not in an MBA program or a Fortune 500 company but in the sweat, blisters, and bloodshed of my first twenty-five working years.

As I built upon those skills, God has allowed me to follow my creative passions—music, drama, film, books—and transform them into lucrative businesses. He has blessed me with a team of individuals who know how to be aware of the timing of investments and to advise me accordingly. In fact, when an acquaintance or reporter asks me what I would be doing if I weren't in the ministry, I tell them that I would probably be doing the same entrepreneurial endeavors that I already do in addition to the ministry, just more of them.

And I tell you all this not to brag, boast, or bully my way into your confidence. However, I want to make it clear that I'm not just some minister who feels led by the Lord to tell you to get out of debt so that you can be a better steward. While this is true—you can be a greater steward for God's kingdom if you're not sinking in a quicksand of debt—I believe that it's for our benefit, not God's, that He consistently emphasizes the importance of avoiding indebtedness. Think about it—God doesn't need our money! He has all the resources of the world, and then some, at His disposal! It's not that He needs my measly tithe or yours to accomplish His divine plans and destinies for all of us. It's that He wants us to be free, to be unencumbered, as we run our race so that we can run faster, longer, and harder than we could otherwise do.

When we take control of our debts and manage our credit responsibly, we liberate ourselves from the slavery of limited opportunities and boundaries set by others. If you truly want to throw off the chains that have inhibited your growth into authentic success, then it's imperative that you include debt management in your equation for repositioning yourself. Have I convinced you to face the giant head on? Then let's go looking for some smooth stones for your slingshot.

Loading Your Slingshot

Two main financial areas support the giant's power source: credit-card debt and mortgage financing. I want us to look at each of these and determine strategies that will enable you to topple this Goliath's hold on your life. We touched on credit-card debt in our last chapter, and I tried to focus on the emotional triggers that likely make it difficult to control spending with our friends Visa, MasterCard, Discover, and American Express, not to mention the credit-card financing available at every major department store, electronics store, furniture store, and even grocery store!

The latest research by the Center for Responsible Lending, a nonprofit and nonpartisan agency committed to fair lending practices and responsible consumer credit, reveals that middle-to-low-income Americans tend to carry a balance on average of $8,650 on their credit cards (www.responsiblelending.org/press/ releases/page.jsp?itemID=28011726). For African-Americans, the news gets even worse. According to a recent study by the Federal Reserve, we typically incur debt representing almost 10 percent of our net worth, while white Americans incur only about 5 percent.

More and more, it seems African-Americans are using credit cards to cover living expenses that should be supported by their income. "Credit card debt has caused African American families to use critical financial resources to pay mounting monthly interest payments instead of saving or acquiring assets such as real estate," observes Aissatou Sidime in a recent article in *Black Enterprise* ("Credit Use Strangles Wealth: African American Debt Is Increasing Faster Than Income," November 2004).

The study by the Federal Reserve also found that more and more minority credit users pay only the minimum amount due each month. As I mentioned in the last chapter, when you are only making a minimum payment, then you are basically doubling the purchase amount of what you buy and extending the payment time long beyond the use of the item and its depreciation. Do you really want to pay over twenty dollars for that latte and coffee cake? Is that blouse really worth the same amount as your car payment?

That's what they become when you charge it and don't pay off the balance.

I realize that credit cannot be avoided in this country, nor should it be. At the risk of repeating myself, you must hear that credit is not a bad thing in and of itself. Like so many resources, all its power results from how it's applied. A fire can provide warmth and a source for cooking your meals or it can devour your home and incinerate all that you've worked hard to accumulate. It's simply a matter of containment and application.

Similarly, you can use credit cards to establish an excellent credit rating, to protect yourself against emergency situations such as car trouble or theft, and to keep track of your expenditures through the itemized statement the company provides. However, the proportions of credit-card spending in our culture have become so epidemic that most people simply resign themselves to being a servant to a faceless master who mercilessly keeps them bound.

Limit the number of credit cards

I once counted the number of credit-card applications that came in the mail to me in one month: seventeen "preapproved" applications, some with credit limits up to $10,000. Since it is so lucrative for banks and other lending institutions to sign up new customers, it's no wonder that they try to make it as easy as possible for you to join the club. Many offer frequent-flier points, a new microwave, a hoodie from your favorite sports team, or some other incentive if you will sign up for a new account. While it appears that these incentive items are free, keep in mind that there's the hidden cost of opening a new account and using it to purchase items you don't really need. If you know that you struggle with controlling your credit spending, then don't be seduced by a free perk that's going to end up costing you hundreds or thousands of dollars in the end.

I would encourage you to keep three credit cards: one for frequent use or daily expenditures that you pay off as fast as possible; one for larger purchases and emergencies that has the best interest rate possible; one that requires you to pay off the balance every month, such as American Express. Many experts encourage you to keep only one card, and while I agree with this advice in principle, I know it's not always practical. Not all merchants accept the same card. Sometimes it's nice to have staggered due dates for payments so that you can pace them with your paycheck. Overall, keep in mind that credit cards are about convenience, not about stealing your own future so that others can get rich while you dig yourself deeper and deeper into a financial grave of high debt.

Don't take it to the limit

Have you noticed the way the credit-card companies typically work? You start out with one credit limit, and as you gradually get closer and closer to that ceiling, they suddenly raise the amount and make more credit available to you. What a wonderful, friendly way to do business, right? Wrong, my friend. You don't need me to point out that this escalation process is designed to get you in the hole deeper and deeper, step-by-step, bit by bit. What starts out as a $2,000 credit limit becomes $5,000. Then the holidays come around and you simply can't resist buying presents for your children, family, and friends. Soon the $5,000 has shot up to a limit of $10,000.

Inch by inch you creep higher and higher until suddenly you find yourself twenty grand behind just by nickel-and-diming your way through life. Basically you end up owing the amount of a car or a down payment on a home. No one reading this would voluntarily say yes, I want to fritter away huge chunks of my future income on disposable items and depreciating assets. Monitor your limits and decide what you want the ceiling to be, not what some actuary calculated using a formula back at the home office.

Change your perception of budget

Often finding a way to control your credit-card use requires a new vocabulary. And it's not just that we need to educate ourselves so that we understand the difference between the prime lending rate and an annual finance charge. Sometimes we must reacquaint ourselves with familiar concepts by using different language.

I know a couple who argued continuously about money. He had one agenda, which basically included enjoying life by spending on whatever he wanted any given day. His wife had another agenda, which included buying their own home and saving enough money so that she could stay home as a full-time mother when they started their family. The B-word got thrown around continuously by each of them with neither really speaking the same language or realizing what it meant to the other. He viewed a budget as a pair of handcuffs intended to restrain his sense of fun and spontaneity. She viewed a budget as a process to ensure fulfillment of future goals.

After they came to me for counseling, it became apparent that we needed a new vocabulary regarding their finances. We decided to replace the B-word with the term *strategy*. Consequently, they each began to realize that *budget* didn't have to be a dirty word or a trigger for misunderstanding. Both acknowledged that they wanted a strategy to use to allocate their financial resources. He began to see that his present happiness was linked to his future freedom. She began to be less preoccupied about the future and to enjoy her husband's fun-loving sense of the present moment.

What are the financial buzzwords that make you cringe every time you hear them? Perhaps start with the B-word. Spend a few minutes describing what you think of and what you feel about the word *budget*. Do you feel guilty, anxious, fearful, frustrated, angry, excited? Something else? Try to be as precise as possible in painting a word picture of your associations with and emotions about this term. At the risk of oversimplifying the complex emotions and experiences that each individual may have with the concept of budgeting, another approach makes it easier to follow a plan.

Interestingly enough, there can be immediate gratification in delaying gratification. Sounds crazy, I know, but if you have a higher goal, a larger purchase, or a bigger dream in mind, then you can focus on that big picture instead of getting sidetracked by your bad mood or the latest weekend sale. Use a budget not to inhibit and restrain yourself but to liberate and unleash your passion for something greater than the purchase that is tempting you in that moment. Do you want to finish your degree? Then plan on how to pay for it. Would you like to own your own home? Then walk by the designer shoes in the store window without a second glance, knowing that walking through the door of your own home is worth more than walking anywhere in those designer leather pumps.

Don't dabble in debit cards without deliberation

It's tempting to believe that debit cards are the way to overcome your bad credit-spending habits because the cash immediately comes out of your account. So if the money's not there, then you can't buy the item. Again, this concept holds true in theory, but in actuality what I've heard from many friends and members of my church is that the debit card feels so much like a credit card that they use it and then end up with no cash in their accounts. While you may feel you're acting responsibly in purchasing the new plasma-screen TV with a debit card, if you now run so close that you can't pay the rent or the car payment, then have you really improved?

If you struggle with overspending on your credit cards, then using a debit card can be a vital part of your deliberate strategy to overcome your problem. But plan far enough ahead so that you can anticipate the needs that you will have and the bills that come due regularly. And don't forget annual or twice-yearly bills such as life, auto, or home insurance, magazine subscriptions, and property taxes.

Debit cards can be a wonderful convenience, and using one is definitely faster than writing a check and in many cases faster than using cash. However, part of your strategy in using one should be identical with the way you use your credit cards. Keep track of your expenditures so that you catch any errors that have been made, but more importantly so that you can see where your money, both present and future, is going.

One woman who attended my Black Economic Success Training (BEST) seminar told me that she never felt that purchasing something with a credit card was real. Since she knew the payment was deferred at least until the end of the month, she never worried about how she would pay. Yet she confessed that this system soon caught up with her and she couldn't ignore the escalating balances. Part of her remedy for this problem was to switch to using a debit card, which instantly deducted the purchase price from her account. This definitely felt more real to her, watching the balance descend item by item.

Do the Math

The single most important step you can take if you want to have financial freedom is purchasing a home. As I've mentioned earlier, African-Americans tend to lag behind their white counterparts in home ownership. But home ownership inevitably encourages two important aspects of wealth building. One is the equity that most homes will automatically build over time. While home prices in some neighborhoods may go up and down, overall, real estate remains the single most lucrative investment you can make. The equity you build by owning a home can later be used to secure a loan for your children's college tuition or to purchase another property.

Moreover, home ownership provides you with an opportunity to borrow a greater amount of money. By making your mortgage payments in a timely fashion, you demonstrate responsible credit management, which only increases the score on your credit rating. A higher score, of course, ensures that you will receive the best rates for whatever you purchase in the future.

Before you jump in, however, and take off for that Realtor's open house around the corner, here are some tips that I've adapted from the Center for Responsible Lending's rules for getting a good home loan.

Be cautious of loans aggressively marketed to niche groups

Often predatory lenders, those institutions intent on exploiting the ignorance and need of those unaware of and unprotected by credit laws, will aggressively market home loans to low-income families, including seniors, single parents, and African-Americans. Most predatory home loans originate from subprime lenders, those who appear to offer a bargain rate but typically create scenarios that often lead to foreclosure. If a lender says that your credit history, including filing for bankruptcy, doesn't matter, this should be a red flag. Your credit history will always be taken into consideration with reputable institutions. You must ascertain the true cost and hidden fees involved in so-called bargain home loans. Predatory lenders frequently use slick sales pitches to skirt around the harsh realities of what they're really selling.

Always shop around and compare traditional lenders' rates with lower-cost lenders before purchasing a subprime loan

Predatory lenders will usually try to sell subprime loans to people who could qualify for an overall lower-cost conventional home loan. People of color are especially susceptible targets for such predators since they know minorities may have difficulty getting a traditional loan or may feel uncomfortable under the intense scrutiny of a traditional lender. In order to ensure that you are receiving the best loan at the best rate given your qualifications, you should compare at least three different lenders' offers. Make sure you have a clear and up-front list of all fees and hidden expenses required throughout the process for each one before making your decision. What sounds like a bargain from the neighborhood accountant may look like a nightmare on paper!

Be realistic about what you can afford short-term and long-term

Most predatory lenders don't care about their customers for the long term; they are primarily interested in getting you signed up right now, today. Don't allow them to talk you into a loan that works now only to end up realizing that interest rates will escalate annually while your chance of unemployment increases. Balloon loans and adjustable-rate mortgages may have enticing "teaser" rates to begin with that allow you to make the initial purchase but then increase so quickly and dramatically that you can't keep up. One expert I know recommends comparing what your monthly mortgage payment is going to be for the first year with what it will be in year five. If the discrepancy is greater than the percentage your income is likely to rise in that time, reconsider your purchase. Generally speaking, your mortgage payment should be no more than 40 to 50 percent of your monthly income.

Make sure you can refinance your home loan without a penalty

Home buyers who go with a higher-interest subprime loan may be eligible for a better mortgage rate with a more stable lender as their credit improves. So it's no surprise that most predatory lenders build in a large prepayment penalty if you pay off the loan early or sell it to another lender. Recent studies show that African-Americans are more likely than others to receive these kinds of prepayment penalties, with many unaware of them until they had signed the papers.

No matter how much you don't like it, do the math

You may hate math, because, let's say, you're a creative type, not a nerd. But I don't care whether that is the case, whether you made bad grades in Algebra I or what, you must do the math, adding up all the fees you'll be required to pay in any given loan agreement to accurately compare the terms and determine which is the better value.

Mortgage percentages or partial percentages paid to the lender, the title company, the Realtor, or other stakeholders, typically called points, are not directly included in your interest rate. For reputable loans, a typical competitive fee will amount to around 1 percent or less of the total loan amount. Predatory lenders, however, will go as high as they can, often as much as 5 percent. You must review the figures ahead of time so that there are no surprises at the table when it comes time to close. Don't hesitate to ask questions and never let anyone rush you through the documents. Keep your calculator handy and, if possible, bring a friend or relative with more financial experience than you.

If you use a broker, make sure you're getting the lowest possible rate

Predatory lenders may utilize mortgage brokers to act as go-between for you and their company. Such brokers have no legal obligation to serve you with the best loan offer; in fact, they typically make more money if the loan costs more. If your lender suggests or requires using a certain broker, then drill deeper into how much such a brokerage service adds to your cost. The best strategy is to avoid such mortgage brokers within the subprime market, the lending arena offering rates lower than prime rate, or else do enough comparison shopping to ensure that you are indeed receiving the lowest possible rates.

Think twice before refinancing

While interest rates remain competitive, it doesn't always mean that you should refinance just because it appears you're getting a lower interest rate. The overall cost could be greater than any short-term benefits. For most of us, our equity (the part of our home we own free of debt) is our greatest asset. Refinances can siphon away our equity to the point where our monthly mortgage may be less but our overall investment in the home is less than it was when we started. If you're inclined to refinance, make sure you shop around the same way you would for a new home loan. You may also want to make sure that you have exhausted other, less expensive options such as a second mortgage or a short-term loan.

Protect your right to go to court

Predatory and less reputable lending institutions will often require you to agree to something known as "mandatory arbitration" rather than the right to a settlement in court. Such arbitrations may not recognize all of your legal rights as a home buyer and may prevent your lender from making full disclosure of forms, records, and fees. You may forfeit your right to appeal if you agree to such arbitration as well. Virtually all financial experts caution against signing anything that binds you to mandatory arbitration rather than legal settlement in a court of law.

Beware of last-minute loan changes

It can be a classic bait and switch or an honest mistake that causes a lender to make last-minute changes at the closing. However, you must not allow yourself to be pressured into accepting any changes that you have not reviewed or do not fully understand. If the terms change or seem different from what you understood them to be, then you must not sign anything until clarity and confidence are restored.

Be Fruitful and Multiply

One of the most compelling reasons to take responsibility for your finances is so that you can pass along a legacy of real wealth to your children and their children. I'm not talking about becoming wealthy and establishing a trust fund, but rather about developing an awareness of how to handle money responsibly and with a balanced attitude.

And just because you didn't inherit a sizable estate or stock portfolio from your parents, don't allow bitterness over the past to eclipse what your legacy can be for future generations. You must keep in mind that God delights in redeeming His children—in buying back that which has been lost, squandered, betrayed, or belittled. Consider how God gave the Hebrews favor to acquire wealth. He used the people who had oppressed them the most—the Egyptians—to get it done. He actually made them reparations for the years of abuse they had endured.

> And I am sure that the king of Egypt will not let you go, no, not by a mighty hand. And I will stretch out my hand, and smite Egypt with all my wonders which I will do in the midst thereof: and after that he will let you go. And I will give this people favour in the sight of the Egyptians: and it shall come to pass, that, when ye go, ye shall not go empty: But every woman shall borrow of her neighbour, and of her that sojourneth in her house, jewels of silver, and jewels of gold, and raiment: and ye shall put them upon your sons, and upon your daughters; and ye shall spoil the Egyptians.
> Exodus 3:19–22 (KJV)

The Hebrews were slaves for four hundred years, and then finally they were having a payday. God transformed their suffering into success. Their oppressors became benefactors, handing over the spoils of Egypt.

Just as the Hebrews experienced, blessings don't necessarily come from nice people. Sometimes great visions are funded by wicked people. Understanding this truth allows us to look beyond the utensil that God used and realize that it was God who blessed us. People are instruments used by God to bless and to direct us into His greater purpose. You will not go out empty!

Just as He delights in remunerating those who were robbed, He also takes great joy in trees that produce good fruit. In fact, one of the things that God abhors the most, stated in both the Old and New Testaments, is anything that isn't fruitful or profitable. And consider how we measure both profit and fruit—they're what you have left when the transaction is over. Whether it's a business deal or a fall harvest, He commands you to have something left. His statement to the children of Israel is that "I will not bring you out of this without filling your empty places." How many times are we willing to walk away from a situation without getting what He has to give us? There is a treasure for every malady you suffered in your life. Do not go out empty! Realize that true treasure may not always be counted in dollars and cents. It may be counted in wisdom and relationships, but you had better know that if God let you go through something, it is because there is a treasure in the dark places in your life.

In the case of the Hebrews leaving Egypt, it was literally a financial treasure. The gross national economy was laid on the backs of the slaves as they escaped the rule of pharaoh. It was easier to get away from his rule than to recover from the debilitating way they had been treated for generations. Those who think a few years of correction fixes decades of abuse are not realistic. The hardest thing for the Hebrews to recover wasn't wealth; it was a healthy self-esteem. They got out of Egypt far quicker than Egypt got out of them. These former slaves were given money, and the first thing they did was spend it on a golden calf.

Giving people money without purpose leads to spenders without direction. What you do with money and where you put it shows a lot about your value system and can help you to recover from the underlying self-esteem issues that result from abuse of any kind.

Perhaps the most important lesson we can learn from both David facing the giant and the Hebrews squaring off against pharaoh is that what we do, we do not only for ourselves but for those who will follow us. How important it is to teach children what it means to be blessed and how to handle finances. Repositioning your children and acclimating them to a new financial environment may be the hardest thing you do. As we change, not only financially but morally and socially, don't forget that the children carry the weight of the changes we make. This is about funding college for the kids. This is about buying learning toys and not just flashy gadgets. This is about planting something in them and not just planting something on them.

A legacy of wisdom and purpose is the wealth you want to leave behind. This is the reason you defeat the giant. So that future generations will have a head start in positioning themselves for greatness, unencumbered by old debts and the ghosts of past Goliaths. Do it for yourself. Do it for your kids. Swing the slingshot with more force than ever before. And release the stone of your determination squarely between his eyes. You will defeat debt and you will be left full!

PART III

Beyond the Limits of Success

INTRODUCTION

And Jesus entered and passed through Jericho. And, behold, there was a man named Zacchaeus, which was the chief among the publicans, and he was rich. And he sought to see Jesus who he was; and could not for the press, because he was little of stature. And he ran before, and climbed up into a sycamore tree to see him: for he was to pass that way. And when Jesus came to the place, he looked up, and saw him, and said unto him, Zacchaeus, make haste, and come down; for today I must abide at thy house. And he made haste, and came down, and received him joyfully. And when they saw it, they all murmured, saying, That he was gone to be guest with a man that is a sinner. And Zacchaeus stood, and said unto the Lord: Behold, Lord, the half of my goods I give to the poor; and if I have taken any thing from any man by false accusation, I restore him fourfold. And Jesus said unto him, This day is salvation come to this house, forsomuch as he also is a son of Abraham. For the Son of man is come to seek and to save that which was lost.

—*Luke 19:1–10 (KJV)*

You likely will not be surprised to learn that the story of Zacchaeus was one of my main inspirations for writing this book. Many of us recall the story of this "wee little man" and his rather unorthodox means of arranging to see Jesus. While reviewing this passage for a sermon, I was struck anew like thunder and lightning from a storm cloud by two truths emerging from it.

First, Zacchaeus had the presence of mind and the forethought to realize that what he wanted—to see Jesus—was not possible from his present vantage point. He had to run ahead and find a new position in order to achieve the desired goal, even if that meant climbing a tree! Can you imagine, as an adult, wanting to see someone so badly that you would act like a ten-year-old again? Keep in mind that Zacchaeus is a rich man, and typically people of wealth dress a certain way and have a certain dignity about them that would preclude them shimmying up a sycamore tree! But this man of little stature seems undaunted and unfazed by what's required to accomplish his goal of seeing the Lord.

Are you willing to humble yourself and do what's required to attain your goal of success in all areas of your life? Will you allow yourself to act like a kid again, to think outside the box and to go beyond the socially acceptable behavior for someone of your stature? Too often we allow our success in life to hem us in and create a new set of limitations that really aren't much different from the old ones, only with more expensive taste! We think that just because we can afford to wear an Armani suit and drive a Mercedes that we no longer need to look ahead and see where we need to be next.

Many people achieve a certain level of prosperity and then find themselves just as unhappy as they were when they were struggling and striving. In fact, many people realize in hindsight that they were happier climbing and clambering than when they arrived at their perceived summit. Zacchaeus compels us to ask ourselves how far we're willing to go to achieve what we really want, which brings me to my second epiphany.

Because of his willingness to reposition himself, Zacchaeus experienced a radical life transformation. He was already successful by the standards of most people both then and now—he was chief among the publicans, a powerful position, as well as rich. He was obviously used to getting what he wanted, with some traits that we can admire, such as his determination, and others that might be questionable, such as falsely accusing others in order to overcharge them. And yet his life was still lacking. He suspected that this man Jesus had something that he needed, something that he couldn't buy in the marketplace or bully others into giving him. Something he wanted desperately enough to run ahead and climb a tree to acquire.

While it's not mentioned in Scripture, I suspect that Zacchaeus may have endured what we often refer to as a midlife crisis. What happens when you achieve all that you've been positioning yourself to accomplish and you still feel empty and incomplete? What does it matter what you have to show for your success if who you truly were meant to be remains hidden?

Zacchaeus has his life transformed through his encounter with the Messiah. After dining and engaging in conversation with Jesus, the tax collector is now willing to give, not the usual tenth for a tithe, but half—50 percent—of his income to the poor! And if he's cheated anyone, well then, he'll refund them four times as much as he took! How we spend our money and how tightly we cling to it provide a clear compass reading on the direction in which our heart is headed. And for Zacchaeus, it's no longer headed in only one direction—toward himself—but toward those around him in need.

My point is not that you need to give away a certain percentage once you attain a certain level of success in order to be happy. No, this generosity is a by-product of the freedom and fulfillment which Zacchaeus experiences in his encounter with Christ. I don't care how often you may be attending church right now, which ministries and charities you may be contributing to, or who you know and consider a spiritual leader. If you haven't encountered Jesus and dined with Him at the intimate table for two inside your heart, then your life will continue to be lacking. If you've reached a certain level of success and realize that your life is still lacking and bound by limitations, then there's a good chance that you might need to visit or revisit the Savior's presence. And you don't have to climb a sycamore tree to do it!

Redeeming Your Losses

Finally, I think it's very telling that Jesus concludes His conversation with Zacchaeus by saying, "For the Son of man is come to seek and to save that which was lost" (verse 10). Repositioning oneself is about experiencing redemption, a word that means to "buy back" or revalue. On our way to the top, en route to the level of success that we believe will satisfy us, we will encounter a number of losses. They may be opportunities and relationships we sacrifice in order to pursue our goal, or they may be losses we suffer over which we have no control.

Regardless how we encounter them, every winner should expect to lose along the way. This is one of the problems I have with the way faith is taught today. We do not prepare people for the fact that faith may not get them a job as quickly as they'd like even if they do pray. This name-it-claim-it idea is dangerous propaganda. It makes people think that success is just a matter of some Easy-Bake recipe—do this, do that, and tell God how you'd like it, when in fact we learn as much about winning by losing as we do from anything else we do. Like a child who stumbles his way into walking, most great people learn what not to do by falling along their way up.

Imagine a little eaglet dumped from the comforts of its nest by its mother. The baby bird initially starts to plummet downward. It flaps its wings a moment and then starts to cascade down again. It is the process of flying and falling that enables it to gain its balance and ultimately soar into heights unknown. Similarly, I can think of few examples of people who didn't fall before they flew.

You may have already had failed relationships. As you read this, you have already sustained damage to a relationship that is important to you. Maybe you have a child with whom you have lost communication and respect. Maybe you have an ex-wife, an estranged friend or lover who just got tired of your obsessive-compulsive work addiction. Maybe they were weary of your distracted grunts at the dinner table or talking to you through newspapers. The good news is that no one lives a full life without losses. It is not the avoidance of failure we are after. It is the inability to learn from the failures that is the most damaging. When you repeatedly fail without learning, then you doom yourself to lunacy—doing the same thing over and over again expecting a different result.

No, you must expect loss in one form or another. Maybe it will be the loss of good credit that you have to bounce back from. Or maybe it is the loss of a job or opportunity, a client or a contract. But all of us lose something along the way. Education is expensive, and often the tuition we pay is not merely to a university or college. Often we pay all along the way through the things we suffer and the pains we endure. In fact, we are billed daily for the tuition of life-loss learning.

Each day we pay for those things we learn, and such lessons

compel us to treasure the success that results from our tenacious pursuit of life. I get concerned when I hear people teaching that faith in God ensures success or that a certain offering alone will guarantee a blessing. The reality is that it takes a combination of faith and works, success and struggles, failures and fortitude, to produce the kind of success that becomes a legacy to be passed on to our children. It is not always what we leave *to* them as much as it is what we leave *in* them. This kind of rich heritage can exist only in the hearts and minds of persons who have sustained and survived losses.

One of the hardest aspects of success is often the perception that truly blessed people have had no losses. People think every deal you did worked. Wrongly they assume that life has afforded you no suffering. Isn't that part of the envy? They think that they had to endure something that you didn't. When in fact what you faced may have been different in nature and detail but just as, if not more, severe than what your envious peers have faced.

No one gets through this world without losses. You know why? It is because life in many ways is a war. And I have never seen a war that didn't leave some casualties along the way. Business, private, personal, emotional—there are all types of ways to incur loss. No one escapes without some damages. No matter which technique you employ, there will be losses. You seek rational reasons for them, when, sometimes, you just lose. It wasn't that you didn't do anything. It's simply a combination of external influences, other people's free will, timing, and happenstance.

Can you imagine going into business and thinking you would have no loss? How many restaurateurs would survive if they didn't expect some food to spoil, some to burn, and some to be taken by dishonest employees and customers? There will be a percentage of bad checks, which is simply the cost of doing business in a corrupt world. Likewise, a banker dares not think that every loan written will be repaid. He cannot think that no house will go into foreclosure. It simply isn't realistic. Given these truths, how can we expect to escape a certain number of losses? To be sure, like all of these examples we can minimize the losses but we cannot totally avoid them. "Be watchful, and strengthen the things which remain, that are ready to die" (Revelation 3:2 [KJV]).

I remember years ago being in a sales-training seminar. The gentleman who taught the class said something I will never forget. He said, "I do not have to teach you how to win. All I have to do is teach you how to face rejection and not give up on winning." Those sales reps who win big are not the ones who are never denied. It is just those who do not allow the "no" of one customer to become a prognosis of fatality. Great salesmen are those who do not allow a "no" to define them. They know that losing is a part of winning.

You will lose time, you will lose good employees, you will lose clients, no matter what you do. If you are a pastor, you will lose members of your congregation. No matter how much we hate the harsh reality, the cruel truth is that our children can die. They can make bad choices even when they have had great role models. Not all relationships can withstand the turbulence of success or the agony of defeat. Some people will lose homes. Some will lose jobs. But it is important to note that the loss of a battle is not loss of the war. Winners have losses. How do they ultimately become winners? They do so by focusing on the leftovers rather than the losses. You cannot land on what you lost. You can only land on what you have left.

What do you do with these losses?

1. Minimize the damage wherever you can.
2. Get some distance, either in perspective or time or both, and reassess what transpired.

3. Make a list of mistakes that contributed to the loss. Note how many of them are in your control and strategize on how you can avoid similar mistakes moving forward.

4. Note how many mistakes contributing to your loss were beyond your control. Chalk them up to the cost of living on the planet.

5. Blame no one. Forgive yourself and others. There's no room for lifelong grudges or guilt complexes in such a short span as a lifetime.

6. Understand that delays are not denials.

7. Make the losses count for something by winning again.

Twelve Feet Tall

Like the limitation of losses, one of the greatest barriers to success can be maintaining the level of your game that got you there in the first place. How does a football team maintain the level of precision and athleticism that won them the Super Bowl the year before? How does an Academy Award–winning actress perform with the same intensity and passion in the film she makes right after she wins the little gold statue? How can a bestselling novelist guarantee that his next novel is as entertaining and as successful as his last? Most times, such success stories don't repeat themselves. Successful individuals build on what they've accomplished, for sure. But they allow themselves the freedom to risk, to reinvent, and to reposition. This is the only way to ensure that they will continue to grow and be truly successful.

So in this final section, I want us to explore some of the ways that our success can begin to slow us down and even cause us to stagnate if we let it. The first two chapters in this section will be addressed specifically to women. It's not that I want to exclude my brothers from our conversation; it's simply that I believe women have achieved a certain level of freedom and power in our culture that has created a new set of success-related obstacles. A woman can now be Speaker of the House, run for president, drive an Indy race car, fly the space shuttle to the moon, or fight in the Middle East. But with this new level of success comes a new set of challenges. These challenges and how to bypass and overcome them form the subject of these two chapters penned "For Ladies Only."

Subsequent chapters will then look at the way our success can create a new set of complications in our relationships. We'll look at how to avoid being successful in our careers at the expense of our personal lives and home life. We'll also consider how to peel away the many labels that others around us will begin to stick on us as we ascend on our path to new heights. Finally, we'll consider what it means to enjoy our success to the fullest, both by embracing our present blessings and by claiming responsibility for the generations that follow.

True success continues growing and developing throughout our entire lifetime. Does an oak tree grow to be twelve feet tall and decide that's high enough so it should stop? Of course not! Like Zacchaeus, we must continually look ahead, aware of what's coming with the next season of life, so that we can reposition ourselves for a happiness unlike any other: the joy that comes from living our life to the fullest as only we can.

eleven

Breaking Glass Ceilings— Sharing the Secrets of Success-Savvy Women

Many women do noble things,
   but you surpass them all.

Charm is deceptive, and beauty is fleeting;
   but a woman who fears the Lord is to be praised.
                                  —*Proverbs 31:29–30 (NIV)*

A shift has occurred in corporate America that allows the doors of opportunity to swing wide for women prepared to enter careers that their grandmothers and great-grandmothers could not have imagined. Women today have worked hard and long to pry open those doors and break through the glass ceiling that once limited their multitudinous talents and abilities. They are pursuing careers in every arena imaginable and performing brilliantly. I shudder to think where our contemporary society would be without their collective brainpower in the workforce.

Who knows how many lives would have been lost if not for the skilled performance of the many female surgeons who have added to the intellectual bank of medical prowess once available only from men. Or how many buildings would be missing from our cityscapes if it were not for the graceful designs provided by female architects? Women who grew up playing with Susie Homemaker sets are now designing space shuttles for NASA. They have put away the hopscotch games of past years and developed computer programs that have revolutionized many industries.

Certainly there are great women and renowned ladies who still find fulfillment in traditional roles of mother and wife; they are the domestic goddesses of someone's dream. There is absolutely nothing wrong with that choice. But women have a choice now and not a sentence given by a jury of men. Irrevocable change has taken place, albeit slowly and gradually.

One need not be a history scholar to know that there was a time in this country when women were not revered or respected as they currently are today. Sexism isn't over any more than racism is over, but we cannot deny that opportunities and attitudes are a lot better today than they were yesterday.

These changes cannot be appreciated without considering how this new climate evolved; the history of this great nation is not without its blemishes. A male chauvinist mind-set was not unusual when this country was founded, but that doesn't exonerate those who considered women little more than property owned by men or kept in waiting for a man to claim. Women who were not chosen by men were mocked as old maids and treated with some disdain even by other women.

The right to vote didn't come easy for women. Women like Susan B. Anthony and Elizabeth Cady Stanton led the way in fighting for long-overdue rights, including the right to vote. They fought ardently and fervently to have a voice in government, not to mention the right to run for office, which wasn't even thinkable at the time of their struggle. Domestic violence did not exist as a term, and men often punished women as if they were children. Women had no rights or privileges. No one to tell, no one to confide in. Most women were not even licensed to drive, with few if any jobs available to sustain themselves.

Money, power, and sex became the bartering tools for those who imprisoned the female in shackles both physical and mental! When Betsy Ross picked up her needles and thread to stitch the flag, she knew that while she could sew it, she couldn't vote for those who would represent it.

If it was a hardship to be a woman, and it was, one can only imagine what befell women of color. Mary McLeod Bethune and other black women were astonishing figures of raw courage. They had two strikes against them, being both black and a woman. Neither could stop them from fighting for the rights that are now almost unnoticed, they are so common. But there was a steep price paid for women's rights to position and reposition themselves in the workplace, in the political arena, in the financial sector, and in every other area imaginable.

Women of the World

Women in our country were not alone in their arduous struggles to be recognized as citizens entitled to the full range of human rights. From the ancient geisha who burned to death, afraid to leave her home without getting permission from the male owner, to the Indian squaw left behind to tend the children and gardens while the men fought and hunted, few cultures really gave woman her due. From the women of China who were sent to other nations COD as mail-order brides to the young ladies of Eastern Europe who were sold as human slaves, most cultures' females have been subjected to some of the worst abuses imaginable. Whether it's physical branding and genital mutilation of African women or Jewish women being raped and debased by their Nazi captors during the Holocaust, half the species has been forced to reposition itself constantly just to survive.

I'll never forget being stunned when I first saw images of female genital mutilations. I was on my first trip to Kenya in an area called West Pekot, where the children performed a play for me that left an indelible impression upon my heart. There we sat, a mere curtain draping us from the relentless rays of the African sun, as the leaders gathered, the men in one area, the children in another, and the women in a third.

I have seen many children in school and church plays, but no past experience prepared me for what they presented to me that day. Dressed in their parents' clothing, the children enacted a most troubling negotiation. In one scene, the father and other men (also played by boys) were bartering for a goat. They spoke in a language that I didn't understand, but an interpreter was at my ear making sure I caught the gist of what these young thespians were saying, that they were auctioning off a handsome young goat.

In the next scene, the boy who played the father in the negotiations was now at home with a girl who played his wife. They were arguing about something. Through my interpreter, I learned it was the mother trying to dissuade him from taking their young daughter away. The "father" finally began to beat his wife with his shoe and run her out of the house, snatching the daughter on her way to school and taking her to the marketplace. There she was handed off like a handful of barley loaves. She was the price he paid for a goat!

I asked the gentleman who translated for me if that was an accurate depiction, and he answered affirmatively. He explained that the purchaser might be a man of fifty or sixty years old. Usually the girl's mother would then prepare her daughter for her new husband by vaginally mutilating her so that her clitoris would be cut away in what is politely called female circumcision but looks—as I saw many horrific pictures of it—more like female castration!

As I am a man with two daughters and as a lifelong advocate for the rights and healing of women everywhere, I was shocked and disgusted by how young girls were denied even the most basic rights of growing up with their organs and passions intact. My physicians, who traveled with me in the country and provided medicine to indigenous people who were without medical services, were telling me how damaging and unhealthy such practices are to the female body. I later learned that many girls bleed to death in the bush from these castrations since they are often performed with such primitive tools as goat horns.

Admittedly, I come from a different culture and may not understand the finer points of this complex ritual. I also understand that not all aspects of this ritual are performed with unsanitary goat horns in the bush. However, based on my observations, research, and extensive questioning of Africans from many tribes, I remain troubled by the way it damages women—creating infection, deteriorating marriages, and endangering childbirth.

The most troubling aspect for me, however, is that, at least in the cases I saw, the procedures are often performed on young girls who are no more than children, often for the benefit of aged men who seek the convenience of controlling the passion of their newly bought brides. I was further appalled to learn that some of the older women not only tolerate the practice but see it as a distinctive honor. Before I left, I encouraged the tribal leaders to allow the girls the hope of a better and more productive life. I challenged them to reconsider ways to honor their rich heritage without endangerment to their girls and to reposition their women for the future of an otherwise wonderful people.

With such an experience fresh in my mind, I was amazed to learn shortly after my visit that at least one African nation had opened its arms to its first female president. I know that this was not a result of my visit but nonetheless this news left me optimistic that all people can change if given a chance. As Ellen Johnson-Sirleaf was inaugurated as the new leader of Liberia, all limitations were broken. I couldn't help but wonder if another young girl somewhere in the bush might be the second president of some other country if positioned properly and given a chance. Now women there, and in fact everywhere, are able to live without the limitations of social bias and indifference based solely on gender. The veil between men and women in that continent got its first rip as she mounted the stage and took the scepter of leadership for the people of her country.

Equal Opportunity Faith

Education and opportunity are the great emancipators in the fight for equality. Education and economic empowerment free more than our checkbook; they open the mind and heart and change the way we process truth. It is true that when people know better, they do better. This is why it is imperative for us to continue to fight to educate people rather than to just evangelize them.

I realize that this statement may raise the eyebrows of some "hellfire and damnation" preachers. But I assure you that the Gospel is more than your favorite three points and a great verse of Scripture at the end. It is more than the head count of so-called conversions collected from decision cards on a missions trip. When Paul says he became all things to all people, he implies that he became enmeshed in the fiber of a culture that he might share his faith in Christ through relationships. We cannot change what we do not understand. I do not profess to fully understand all the nuances of culture, but I want to see culture preserved without the perpetuation of female degradation. And by God's grace, it can be done.

True religion, good religion, has a responsibility to do more than sit idly by and watch people be abused and only offer the sinner's prayer. I love to see people saved, but too often the salvation of a person is focused only around his confession. The true salvation of a society has more to do with economics, ethics, education, and a strong sense of God's creative plan for all his beings.

I still remember as a little boy watching women come to the pulpit as ushers to bring water to the preacher, and he would come to the edge and get it, since they were not allowed to walk into the pulpit that they had raised the money to build. I can remember the times when women were not allowed to speak or read anything from behind the "sacred desk" simply because they were women. And yet men of notable as well as questionable character were welcomed into the pastor's office and allowed to preach sermon after sermon simply because they were men.

In many churches, the women who made up the vast numbers in the congregation were not always treated with real respect. They were left behind, waiting for doors to open, waiting for years. Many died without ever being treated as more than second-class citizens all in the name of keeping the pulpit pure and free of the contamination of female presence. I realize that the idea of women preaching is controversial in some religious circles. I do not agree with those who do not support women in ministry, but that is their right. It goes much deeper than preaching. I can recall few or no major roles given to women in any area of leadership in the church as I was growing up.

This was an era when a well-dressed woman had to wear gloves. I know that in admitting this, I have dated myself! But perhaps you remember when it was almost a sin to wear a felt hat after the first day of spring. Or, God forbid, a straw hat after Labor Day! These were the days when the civil rights struggle was on the front pages of prestigious black publications like *Jet* and *Ebony*. It was a time when the pillbox hat graced a lady's head, rouge (not then called blush) adorned her cheeks, and she smelled of Avon's Honeysuckle! It was an important era. It left an indelible impression on me, and even writing this brings the faint smell of Bergamot hair grease to my nostrils and the memory of hot combs on the kitchen stove!

These attitudes toward women in the church did not begin with the old "colored" churches (as they were called during that time) that I grew up in, although they were sadly perpetuated by such churches. With the open windows, hymnals stacked in seats, Martin Luther King Jr. fans clutched in praying hands, the church body kept praying and fanning, sweating and praying, but rarely utilized the tremendous brain trust of women who were relegated to the tasks of washing the pillowcase-covered seats in the choir stand and baking the sweet-potato pies that would be sold for the Pastor's Aide. There was so much more that they were gifted and prepared to offer, but most churches withheld from women the right to administrate or govern as well as preach.

Divine Intervention

Many strides were made at the time, but the church struggled then, and still does even now in some circles, to understand its need to serve its constituency and support the dreams of those who support it. Though I know all churches were not like the ones from my boyhood, many were then, and a few still are today. We can observe traces of this kind of discrimination in the Bible and its approach to disputes between genders.

Remember the daughters of Zolophehad? They were women who traveled with the children of Israel who had no brothers but fought for the right to be acknowledged as legitimate heirs to their father's legacy (see Numbers 27:1–11). Even Moses was uncomfortable with giving them this honor, which was traditionally reserved for men. The Bible says that it took God speaking directly to this great leader to make him realize that the women were right! Their women were gladiators of faith who refused to be relegated to a position of inferiority and prevailed after divine intervention. Sometimes it takes divine intervention for justice to prevail! Divine intervention and a lot of human tenacity make for a great combination in a fight for the freedom of any oppressed people. To be sure, Moses was a great leader and a man of God, but when it came to his views on women, he was wrong!

Or what of the great debate that existed in Jesus' day when the men brought the woman taken in adultery to be stoned? They dragged her into the streets of Jerusalem to stone her for an act that, no doubt, many of them had privately enjoyed. That is how religion can be. It is often riddled with double standards, as men contaminate God's plan for wholeness with cultural biases and scriptural misinterpretations. It is not that they don't have scriptural support for their bigotry. Men always find Scriptures to support the acts they want to perpetrate against one another. My question is not whether they had the right to stone her. But how can you stone the woman caught in the act of adultery and totally ignore the man? If she was caught in the act, she wasn't there by herself. But when men judge, they often do it with a double standard. If a man makes a mistake, he is often punished with a slap on the hand. But if a woman gets caught, she is branded with a scarlet letter and condemned to public execution!

Too often institutions, including the church and political bodies, love principles more than people, ceremony more than service, condemnation more than comfort, and the results are catastrophic! To be sure, the religious world has often controlled women, covering more than their heads. Some religions helped to cover the minds of bright women with rules that ultimately denied them education and privilege. In 1 Corinthians 11:13–16, the apostle Paul among other issues grapples with women having their heads covered and other social conventions of the time that drew a sharp line of demarcation between how women and men were expected to behave. His ideas, like those of many leaders today, were based on ideas of the times in which he had to minister. Admittedly, it is difficult to find your voice when you stand alone on an issue and so many respected people oppose you. I understand that many ministers, myself included, wrestle with when and when not to take on an issue like women's rights. Culture and religion, along with politics and religion, often make strange bedfellows.

May God give us courage today to tackle tough subjects based not on trends but on truth. While some male leaders fight about women's rights and other issues, they often do so in a way that concerns what is considered culturally or politically correct at the moment rather than with a Christ-like desire to liberate the captive. In reality, whether you are taught to walk behind the man, as some cultures teach, or denied an education, as women used to be denied and sometimes are still denied, our daughters and sisters are treated as less than man. Regardless of what the details are, the effects are the same—to impose inferiority and to keep women somehow subservient!

Understanding the great forces that oppose female emancipation, it is important that women today seize the new opportunities and with all diligence advance forward. Today is a new day for women. It is against the dismal backdrop of religion and history that we see women emerging today.

Whole Lot of Shaking Going On

Equally important as the opportunities now afforded you is the matter of assuming new positions with grace and focus. It is hard for those who fight their way up not to become corrupted by the fight they had to undertake in order to get there. Yet it is important that you remain upwardly mobile without becoming infected with cynicism. It is not easy to be better without becoming bitter about how long it took and what you endured along the way. However, bitterness is a great deterrent to creativity and can linger like poison in the system of a heart that is bruised by a grievous blow to the soul.

If Elvis could see the landscape of our society today, he would tell you our homes as well as our workplaces are all shook up. I mean really shook up, with some serious fallout. But that is generally the case when a major realignment takes place. Let me illustrate with one of the best examples that I've experienced.

I was invited a few years ago to watch a basketball game at the American Airlines Arena in Dallas. The Lakers were playing the

Dallas Mavericks, and boy, it was quite a game. I brought my family and we had a ball. Afterward I was invited by a friend to meet some of the Lakers back in the locker room. Now, I am not a sports buff, but even I wasn't about to miss the opportunity to meet guys like Shaquille O'Neal and Dennis Rodman even if I had to do it in a sweaty locker room. So I anxiously and excitedly went back there to meet the guys, who had largely stripped down, amid a sea of sweat and hair. As we were chatting briefly, and one player after another was going in and out of the shower, coaches were whispering about who did and didn't do well, and I was trying to figure out a nice spiritual way to get an autograph for my daughters, who were waiting outside. It was for them—really it was! Anyway, I hadn't gotten up my nerve to ask; I didn't want to look like a groupie or, worse still, a stalker! Suddenly the door swung open and in came both men and women reporters with cameras to do interviews. I was shocked! Female journalists breezed through a locker room full of men who were scantily dressed, if at all.

I got out of the way as the interviews commenced, but as my friend walked me back to my family I asked what the women were doing in the locker room while the men were dressing. A high-ranking member of the Mavericks management said that the women who were with the press had fought for the right to have equal access to the men for interviews and won it. Now, today, behavior that once would have gotten a man arrested or at least his face slapped—I'm talking about walking into a room reserved for seminaked women—has been turned upside down . . . and the face slapping occurs if women are denied the right to walk into a room full of seminaked men!

I recall this story only to reinforce the fact that there's a whole lot of shaking going on. The world's views on many things are changing. When all is said and done, I am not sure what it will look like. But as I drove home from the ball game that evening, I knew this was not Kansas, Dorothy. This was definitely not my father's world!

Warm-Up Exercises

Just as changes in the roles of men and women have been made all around us, you must ask yourself what changes are you making within. Which values will you hold on to and which are you willing to lose in order to attain the next stage of life? These are hard questions with no right or wrong answer. But they are questions that require your thoughts and plans in order to maximize the time in history that you have been chosen to live in.

Anytime there is a shift like we're experiencing, we will spend years in a state of tremors and fallout from the realignment. Your repositioning has a huge impact on the whole family. Children are affected. Men and women, themselves, are often asking how a "lady" should now be treated. When is he being respectful; when is he being condescending? How do you tell when he's being chivalrous and when he's being patronizing? There are no easy answers; you must examine each and every situation and the nature of your relationship. Now men and women both stand at the door of the office wondering who should open it first.

Etiquette is being rewritten, the word *harassment* has taken on a new meaning, training books for office protocol and politically correct phrasing are everywhere. One woman says, "I can open the door for myself, thank you." The other one says, "I may be at work, but I still want to be treated with the social graces that I am accustomed to." And the men are just standing there bewildered. So, sister, have a little mercy on a brother and give him a chance to figure out whether he should tip his hat or hang his head. Should he be scrupulously polite when you join him for dinner, or treat you like one of the fellas? Often women do not agree on protocol, so no wonder men are scratching their heads! The world is in transition, and as is the case in any transition, every gimme has a gotcha. We will gain some things we didn't have, but lose some good things we will regret!

Most important is that you realize that revolution is well under way, and you need to reposition yourself for both the opportunities and the liabilities. Training your daughters for new-world ideas is as important as training sons for the vital roles they can play in this new era. I personally think many men are struggling with their identity, which was historically built on providing and leading in the home. Today that role is being devalued by an ideology where women compete with men rather than completing them, in loving relationships.

Yes, we do have some bugs to iron out, but during this process there are some steps you can take, married or single, young or old, to prepare you for the doors that are opening before you today. Much like the stretches and warm-up exercises that we do prior to a vigorous workout, these tips will help you to build strength and agility as you prepare to run a new stretch of your journey on a much wider road.

1. Given that women often live longer than men and more women are not marrying until after age thirty, women need to plan on being financially independent. Finding the right Blahniks to go with that Prada dress is not as important as finding the right investment plan to prepare you for the future. Take charge of your retirement today, right now. Don't rely on him or the man you might meet.

2. Realize that you may need to change horses in the middle of

the race to get to the finish line in good shape. By this I mean give yourself the freedom and flexibility of thought to change careers if the path you are on now does not transport you to where you want to be in twenty years. Depending on your age and ability, you can start over again and regroup for the open doors that were not there twenty years ago when you chose to do what you are now doing.

3. Do the research necessary to ensure that you receive the respect you deserve where you shop. This means that when you pick out a car, also pick out a dealership whose service department has a sound reputation for treating women just as fairly as men. Rather than spending your precious time arguing with a service provider who treats you like "the little woman" on *Little House on the Prairie,* find someone who does not insult your intelligence or exploit your checkbook.

4. Develop hobbies that put you in the company of the people with whom you want to be associated. Especially since most men do business outside of the office, being good in the boardroom might not be enough. A sister may have to take a few golf lessons to get into the real game!

5. Make sure you have an insurance policy that covers your mortgage if you become ill, incapacitated, or otherwise impaired. Since you may not have a companion, you have to have a backup plan. Don't wait until the crisis and wonder why you aren't sheltered from the storms. Look ahead and prepare a safe harbor where you can recover if you ever falter physically or emotionally.

6. Don't embrace new trends just for the sake of being hip and contemporary. There is nothing wrong with holding to the traditional values that are important to you. This is not about being new for the sake of being new. It is more an expression of

the new options. You can pick and choose much the way you do when you coordinate a wardrobe, choosing the things that fit you and do not limit you! Like having your cake and eating it, too, you can have the best of both worlds.

7. Teach your daughters the technology of the times so that they can navigate in a contemporary society. (Or in some cases, ask them to teach you! Often our children are learning how to utilize technology before we do, so don't be shy about asking for help if you need it.) Learn and teach decisiveness, negotiation, sound ethical business principles, and business acumen. These are the tools necessary for success and repositioning.

Now as never before there is a door being opened to you. It is your time to walk through it. Prepared for both the progress and the process of being new and fresh, you are ready to reposition yourself into the sweet spot of life, where you can peel off the dead layers of past cultural and sexist limitations, revealing the radiant power of who you are. This is your time for innovative thinking without losing traditional values! You are woman, and I hear you roaring and raring to go!

twelve

Shattering Glass Slippers—Revealing More Secrets of Women's Success

The wise woman builds her house,
  but with her own hands the foolish one tears
  hers down.

—*Proverbs 14:1 (NIV)*

Arecently crowned beauty queen made all the headlines with her wild party-girl antics involving underage drinking, revealing more of herself than is considered decent in public, and even kissing another beauty pageant winner! She teetered precariously close to losing her crown and its benefits before being given a second chance by pageant officials. This woman who won like Cinderella in a night of overwhelming success almost lost it all. Instead of regal poise and all-American pride, she left an image of a fallen princess stumbling out of her glass slippers and leaving her coach smelling like a rotten pumpkin. Donald Trump became the prince charming who rescued the tarnished damsel in distress, and with great chivalry gave her a second chance.

Needless to say, the media went wild. A journalist covering the story commented that most beauty queens fade from our memories faster than the name of our waitress at lunch yesterday. The ones who remain in the public eye are the young women whose bad behavior—whether it's posing for men's magazines in ways that are inappropriate, or falsifying their résumés—transforms their fifteen minutes of fame into infamy. Unfortunately, there's some truth to what this reporter observed. Despite the failure of these ladies to serve as role models we want our daughters and nieces to emulate, we can definitely learn something from them.

Giving the Grace to Grow

Celebrities are just as human as you and me. They are no more entitled to, or exempted from, the consequences of outrageous behavior than anyone else. As was the case with the beauty queen incident, we constantly hear about an Academy Award winner arrested for drunk driving, a comedian making a racist remark, or a celebrity participating in insider trading. And more times than not, the public is very forgiving and willing to allow these performers a second chance.

This is where I believe we can learn from them: it doesn't seem to hurt their level of success. It's not just that they learn something from their mistake (even if it's only how to avoid being caught by the paparazzi the next time!). They are forced to reposition themselves after the scandal. After having metaphorically tripped on their way out of the ladies' room with their fine Italian stilettos trailing toilet paper, these women get up and get on with where they're headed.

There are two lessons that can be learned from such awkward and unfortunate situations. One is we apply a double standard to the celebrity miscreants and those who have erred in the church. We have in our Bible all of these great words like *redemption, reconciliation, restoration, revival,* and *renewal,* but, when one of our highly notable or even not so highly notable persons has a mishap, we banish them. Perhaps depending on the details, it may not be wise to restore a person immediately to a position of high authority. But why would we not allow them to be redeemed, restored, or *repositioned*? Instead we feed them to the lions in the press and elsewhere. The anxious and sometimes biased world is always ready to devour a fresh morsel of failed spiritual character. It is true that the "secular" are always there to criticize the failures of the "sacred," and sometimes we earn that scorn. But when jewelry made of secular gold is tarnished in the oxidizing environment of carnal debauchery, it can seemingly rebound more readily than the jewels that ornament religious crowns. When secular leaders or celebrities, counselors, and professionals have these embarrassing mishaps, they are rehabilitated; they reposition themselves, and move on to their next endeavor. However, when we of the church are in the same situation—and we are no more exempt from the pitfalls of our humanity than anyone else—we are cremated!

Granted, there are times when dealing with a situation in the church when it becomes absolutely and undeniably appropriate to remove an individual. As in the case of pedophiles in church leadership and other parasitic individuals who resist reform. They must be confronted and must not be allowed to lead or serve where children and other church members are put at risk.

However, there should be a distinction made between how we handle weakness as opposed to wickedness. The first is an opportunity to exhibit God's redemptive grace and allow the same blood that flows from the pulpit to flow to it. But the latter continues to remind us of God's judgment. Both are aspects of who He is and how He moves.

Nowhere is this better illustrated than when Jesus through an angel sends for Peter, whose discipleship was marred by a complete denial of the Lord. Yet Jesus sends for him and forgives him, releasing him to serve his Church with dignity and grace.

If you are one of those who have been tossed into the garbage and you feel like you are headed for the incinerator, this may be the redeeming moment that repositions you from the junkyard to the recycle shop. As long as the church destroys our flawed persons, we will perpetuate the myth that the rest of us are spotless.

Like the would-be righteous who came to stone the woman caught in the act of adultery, we all soon realize that we are no better or worse than the ones we criticize. We know deep down we have no rocks to throw, and worse still, we deny ourselves the chance to study and grow from working with people who could give us a template for recovery. We muffle out the voices of those who have been there, done that, and try to impress a busy world that has gone on to the next story with how sternly we hold our ideals.

The first lesson that we all need to absorb is how to rebound from mistakes and reposition our lives into power again. How do we bring ministry out of misery? Secular institutions such as Alcoholics Anonymous and the Betty Ford Clinic with their wide array of recovery treatments and facilities are ahead of the sacred, which have very few options that offer second chances for anyone. If you don't offer these to the highly visible, then you advertise no mercy to the less visible who are watching from the sidelines of the stage. Unfortunately, this is nothing new: "For the people of this world are more shrewd in dealing with their own kind than are the people of the light" (Luke 16:8, NIV).

Second, we must learn what happens on the stage of life that causes even the well intended to trip, fall, or stumble in the spotlight of great opportunities. I am saying simply that forgiveness leaves a message. Donald Trump and his fallen beauty queen, regardless of the ultimate outcome, leave us a life lesson that ladies must embrace and use to empower themselves toward a life without limits: You can *always* begin again.

Frequently in my church ministry, conferences, and *Woman, Thou Art Loosed!* events, I encounter women carrying enormous loads of guilt, shame, anger, fear, and anxiety over the abusive pasts that continue to haunt their present and to inhibit their future. Many of these ladies, no matter how successful they may be in terms of careers and families, view themselves as victims and failures rather than as strivers and survivors. As if it were not enough to have to find the strength to survive an often unforgiving world, they have the added burden of surviving their own remorse, shame, and guilt.

They can't see beyond their pain and the limitations of their own blindsided perceptions to realize that they can release the burdens of the past and continue their journey at a new pace with a lighter load. They haven't grasped what Jesus meant when He said, "My yoke is easy and my burden is light" (Matthew 11:30, NIV).

But the truth really can set you free. And here's the truth: It doesn't matter what you've done, who's hurt you, or whom you've hurt, it's not too late. I don't care what you've done or haven't done, whom you've been with and whom you've walked out on, you can reposition yourself beginning right here, right now. It will not be easy, but I know it can be done and I know that you can do it.

Among the most common things women offer as an excuse for not releasing the burdens of their past is "This is who I am." But I often share with them that no true winner can allow one or even a few mishaps to define who she is. You can't define yourself by what you did. Often there is a great gulf between who we are and what we did. Or they will say, "This is how people know me. They won't let me break out of the way they know me." While there's some truth to the way that the perceptions and attitudes of others can hinder us as we reposition ourselves, you would be surprised how willing and eager those around you can be when it comes to allowing you to change.

If we are willing to demonstrate how we have changed not just by what we say but what we do, then others will often allow us to restore their trust. We may need to apologize, to restore, and to make amends to be taken seriously, but if we sincerely move in a new and better direction, others will notice. We don't have to scream from the rooftops how much we've changed—our actions will speak louder.

Still certain people may try to lock you into an old role or to define you by a past mistake. These men and women display their own insecurities when they won't allow you to transform yourself and move on. But these naysayers will definitely be in the minority, so do not focus your energies on arguing with or refuting them. Instead pour your energies into repositioning yourself into a woman who may have a tarnished past but who has a twenty-four-karat future!

You Can Have It All

A friend of mine, an author whose insightful relationship-advice books linger for months on the bestseller charts, is an Ivy League graduate, married to a man who adores her, and the mother of two healthy, beautiful children. Her calendar of speaking engagements is booked up a year and a half in advance. By all accounts, she is the epitome of a successful modern woman.

We recently shared the podium at a conference where the opportunity arose for her to confide in me that she is miserable. She told me that her life feels so out of balance that she's not sure how to get it back to normal. That led to a conversation between us about having it all.

She flies between two and four times a week. The other days she writes her books and columns, conducts research, oversees her small staff, and tries to squeeze in time for her husband and children. She made me feel like a slacker for sleeping five hours a night. All of this activity has taken a toll and left her weary-eyed and with a halfhearted smile.

Like many women in her shoes, she can have it all, just not all the time. She has to allow herself time to rest and recover. Like many men and women who bring home the bacon and fry it up in a pan, she is stressed to such a degree that it could kill her. She is also finding herself with more things in common with men than just job and salary. In the past, women have tended to outlive men because they were not subject to as much on-the-job stress. This is no longer the case. Stress is a killer, leading us to eating disorders, soaring depression rates, unstable relationships, and extramarital affairs.

I'm warning you here about the side effects of greatness and the pitfalls of having it all, all the time. Please allow yourself a space, a pause, a tranquil moment to spiritually replenish yourself on a regular basis. When you give yourself the refreshing nourishment of peace and solitude, you are better able to forgive yourself when you make mistakes, be more forgiving of others, and create an atmosphere of calm sobriety. You'll be better able to strategize, and develop your safety net called repositioning, so that, if the bottom falls out of your home life, finances, or career, you'll have something in reserve for an emergency landing. The safety net is learning the ability to reposition yourself even if you do suffer a fall.

Repositioning has turned fallen beauty queens into movie stars, ex-rappers into talk-show hosts . . . former talk-show hosts into actors, former actors into politicians—the list is endless. It relieves a certain amount of stress anytime you are falling off the high wire just to know that there is a well-tied net awaiting you below. The wind may be whizzing by you, your limbs twisted like a pretzel, and your face may be grimacing like a Halloween mask, but as long as you land in the net, you can eventually regain your composure. Leaping up into a bouncing position, you then give a struggling smile to the audience, listening as their screams of horror become cheers of joy.

The net for you may be an alternative plan, a contingency plan. The bottom line is, stuff happens!

My mom used to move a plant from one location to another. Whenever she did so, it was because the way the plant was doing was disappointing her, and she knew that actions were better than agony. Sometimes she would have to transplant the struggling plant from one pot to another. Other times, a slight adjustment from an east window to a west one was all it took. Small adjustments can make massive differences. My mom's ability to sense when the plant had outgrown its environment or wasn't getting the light it needed had an amazing effect on the plant. We said she had a green thumb. What she really had was a great instinct for when to do what was needed. Do you have that? If so, how are you using it to further your objectives?

If there is one thing I have learned about women, it is that you are all innately sensitive. Don't ignore your instincts and be left to the limitation of facts alone. Facts can often point to things that are not true. Just as circumstantial evidence in a criminal case may not be enough to warrant prosecution. Sometimes you cannot make a decision with the facts alone. Listen to your instincts. They brought you to where you are. Do not forsake them. Consider the facts but include the instincts also.

This is what my mother did with her green thumb. Our once-ailing greenish-brown agricultural disaster would turn into a beautiful plant, blossoming and emitting delightful fragrance because something instinctively told my mother that change was the only way to salvage it.

I probably would have thrown the plant away, but she repositioned it and it thrived again, even after a past failure. If you understand that your safety net is there just in case your performance or the tautness of the wire or even the agility of your partner has set you up for a fall, then you know you will bounce back. With a net, you may as the Bible says "fall but you will not be utterly cast down"! Got it? Good, then we're now ready to discuss that "other" item you need to survive the high wires and low landings of life.

Beauty in the Balance

I want to share some thoughts with you on the beauty of a balanced woman. There is nothing more beneficial to herself and to those around her than to be a woman who is balanced and not moving to extremes. Some of our best role models are seen in the successful women of the Bible, particularly the wonder woman described in Proverbs 31. In this passage of Scripture, we find numerous attributes used to describe a multitalented woman who has come into her own. Let's consider just a few of these:

> She selects wool and flax
>> and works with eager hands.
> She is like the merchant ships,
>> bringing her food from afar.
> She gets up while it is still dark;
>> she provides food for her family
>> and portions for her servant girls.
> She considers a field and buys it;
>> out of her earnings she plants a vineyard.
> She sets about her work vigorously;
>> her arms are strong for her tasks.
> She sees that her trading is profitable,
>> and her lamp does not go out at night.
> In her hand she holds the distaff
>> and grasps the spindle with her fingers.
> She opens her arms to the poor
>> and extends her hands to the needy.
> When it snows, she has no fear for her household;
>> for all of them are clothed in scarlet.
> She makes coverings for her bed;
>> she is clothed in fine linen and purple.
> Her husband is respected at the city gate,
>> where he takes his seat among the elders of the land.
> She makes linen garments and sells them,
>> and supplies the merchants with sashes.

She is clothed with strength and dignity;
>   she can laugh at the days to come.
She speaks with wisdom,
>   and faithful instruction is on her tongue.
She watches over the affairs of her household
>   and does not eat the bread of idleness.
Her children arise and call her blessed;
>   her husband also, and he praises her:
"Many women do noble things,
>   but you surpass them all."

>   Proverbs 31:13–29 (NIV)

Said to be about the mother of King Lemuel, a leader about whom we know little other than the fact that his mother set high standards for his wife, this passage might intimidate you at first. For one thing, this description is over two thousand years old, but it sounds remarkably contemporary! Like my friend the successful speaker and author, you might believe that yes, you can have it all, but that the price is so steep that you will simply be trading one set of worries and stressors for another.

But I don't believe that to be the case. Certainly the woman described here is a stunningly successful multitasker. But keep in mind what is missing from this description as well: how long it took her to find a husband, how many times she failed in her various endeavors, and what she learned from those mistakes. In many ways, what we see here in Proverbs 31 is simply a résumé that displays her greatest strengths. As you certainly know, you don't compose a résumé listing the worst of your traits.

Let's look at a few select qualities from this list. This woman is clearly hardworking: she's busy with selecting, spinning, and weaving wool; she keeps a garden and vineyards; she sells her handmade goods in the marketplace; she oversees a household that includes a husband, children, and staff ("servant girls"). She's also a savvy real-estate investor who plans ahead and gives generously to those around her who are in need. She plans for the seasons and always dresses beautifully. She's much beloved and well respected. Overall—and this is what I would emphasize here for us today—her life is integrated.

It's no accident that the words *integrate* and *integrity* are derived from the same root, the Latin *integrare*, meaning "to make whole," which, I believe, is really just another way of saying balanced. This is the element that my successful female friend was lacking in her life. She had a very overdeveloped career and professional life and a very underdeveloped and rarely enjoyed personal life. She was dancing on a high wire with one foot! There was no longer any fun and satisfaction in her success because in order to work hard enough to sustain it, she was forced to sacrifice the catalyst for her success: her own sense of a healthy self.

Those women who seem so successful in our eyes—the ones who would make King Lemuel's mother proud, the ones who seem truly joyful and at peace with themselves even as they run their own business as well as their families—have one thing in common. They're integrated. They have an integrity about who they are and what they do, no matter what they're doing. Whether she's leading a conference call with the corporate executives in an international division or preparing a holiday dinner for the extended family, there's a quality to it that makes it her own. We can call it grace, or poise, or charm, but the reality is that it's her own brand of giving who she is and what she's about.

Successful actresses often employ a variety of methods for getting into the various characters they play. From makeup and costuming to voice coaches and accents, all the details converge and are integrated into her performance. If you consider the many talented actresses who continue to excel in their craft, you might notice that they often shine in their ability to play very different and disparate characters. From a maid to a madame, from a pirate to a princess, these performers can transform their characters into plausible individuals who compel us with their complexity. However, I would argue that no matter how successfully an actress convinces us that she's another person, something emerges from all of her performances that makes them uniquely her own.

Similarly, the same could be said of a painter—all of Grandma Moses' lovely primitives share commonalities just as those by Georgia O'Keeffe are united by elements that emerged from the core of who she was. Potters develop individual artistic styles and traits that are displayed in their pottery. Jewelry makers and seamstresses as well. You see, all of us are artists of life, continually refining and integrating our abilities to produce our truest and most beautiful creations. It's how we're made by a loving Creator and it's how we best learn to live successfully: in a manner that's balanced and integrated, focused but not finalized, at peace with ourselves in a way that liberates all the talents within us.

Add a Little Seasoning

After integration, another characteristic that I believe the woman from Proverbs 31 offers for emulation is her ability to sustain momentum. Now, I realize that by viewing her as a woman who learned to master momentum, I am inferring something about her from her scriptural portrait. Like a crime-scene investigator adding up clues, I'm deducing that in order for this woman to be as good as she is at so many diverse interests and business endeavors, she must know how to use her energy and her awareness of time and season to her advantage. She knows when to plant seeds and when to harvest the grapes. She knows when to collect wool and when to spin it. She knows when to make a garment and when to sell it. She knows when to make money and when to give it away.

Along with living an integrated life, she is in sync with the flow of the seasons and aware of their impact on her and her circumstances. She reminds me of a lovely woman on the dance floor whose body is in sync with her mood and with the music. She's not trying to upstage anyone else; she may not even have a partner with whom to share the pulsing beat of the music. She could be married or single, a mother or a sister, but she's fully alive to the music and fully present to who she is in the moment.

Athletes like my friends Michael Irvin and Emmitt Smith call this being "in the zone" or "in the flow." In fact, I believe that one of the key reasons that Emmitt was able to transform his footwork on the football field into fine moves on *Dancing with the Stars* is that he instinctively knows what it means to find the rhythm of the moment. If a play on the gridiron had to be changed at the last minute in order to counter a defensive strategy suddenly revealed on the field, Emmitt knew how to adjust the tempo. Similarly, he could go from a tango to a two-step, a fox-trot to a waltz, with the ease of someone who's flexible and adaptable to the music that life sends his way.

What kind of dancer are you? Have you experienced moments or seasons in your life when you knew that you were exactly where you should be? How far are you from being in such a place right now? What is keeping you from being in sync with the present season of your life? Of course, this begs the question, How would you describe the present season of your life? Are you bounding into the new life and rebirth of who you are like a rabbit in the springtime?

Or are you experiencing the peak of your career in a blistering summer climb up the corporate ladder? Maybe there's a slowdown moving your way, an autumnal time to step back and observe the beauty of where you've been and where you're going next. Balance yourself, balance your successes, put the other foot down, and get a pedicure for God's sake! Spend an evening at the museum or the spa. Balance is a part of your safety and integrating it ensures wholeness. Perhaps it feels like a snowy, arctic cold front has enveloped your emotional and circumstantial landscape right now, freezing you in a winter chill. It is just God's way of warning you that you need to come in out of the cold and integrate more variety into your life.

As we've already established, knowing where you are in the present is vital if you are to reposition yourself for the next season of life. And keep in mind that while our natural seasons follow a regular order—winter, spring, summer, fall—our personal seasons may vary considerably. I've had many springtime sprouts snuffed out by a bitter-cold frost. I've also seen a fall harvest leave a large bounty behind it.

So living in the rhythm of where you are and preparing for your next season does not necessarily mean keeping your winter coat handy just because it's January. You must be adaptable and ready to seize an opportunity when it comes your way. You must know when to hibernate and stay away from last year's spring fling and when to risk blazing your own trail along uncharted territory. You need to ask yourself if a particular harvest is worth investing so much of your energy to produce. You must pay attention to when you need rest and when it's worthwhile to push yourself through the tired barrier in order to accomplish your goal.

Self-awareness and the questions you ask yourself are crucial to this process of monitoring your internal momentum. If you've committed to staying at home and raising the kids, then it may not be the best time to start your own business. Maybe you can lay the groundwork while they're small so that by the time they enter school and your schedule becomes more flexible you can launch an entrepreneurial venture. Or if you've finally reached a level of success where your company provides you with a month's vacation, then you need to take it. It's likely that your employers know that the intense level of engagement your work requires necessitates that you rest and recover regularly if you are to avoid burnout.

Most people I talk to about mastering their momentum, particularly women, who are often intuitively aware, tell me that the seasonal signs are often obvious. They simply choose to ignore them or deny them or try and impose their own agendas on them. But just as a storm front moving in over the plains with its forty-mile-per-hour winds, sheets of rain, and deadly lightning cannot be ignored, neither can certain realities in your life.

Don't be afraid of embracing your present season, even if it's one that you don't particularly enjoy or want to acknowledge. You may be going through a season of grief or transition that is particularly painful right now. Instead of fighting this season and the cues it's providing you right now, allow yourself to experience what it has to offer, knowing that it's preparing you for a richer season ahead. Even the ground must be allowed time to lie fallow in order that its nutrients and minerals will be replenished. Only then can it return with a new healthy crop that lives up to the land's full potential.

As we close this chapter, like King Lemuel, I am searching. Searching for a woman who is ready to step into her destiny, armed with the tools she needs to succeed. She has to be clear on her seasons, convinced of her contribution, aware of her own frailties, and flexible enough to adapt to unexpected setbacks. If you are such a woman, know such a woman, or are the lucky man who is married to her, then please let her know that she lives in a generation where the glass ceiling has been turned into a glass slipper. If she has the courage to believe, nothing shall be impossible for her. I want her to know that there are no limitations even when there have been past mishaps and agonies. This is a new day with new opportunities. She may have to rest sometimes, pray sometimes, forgive sometimes, and, yes, even fight sometimes. But like Cinderella, if the shoe fits, wear it!

thirteen

Mail Carriers—Surviving the Labels of Success

> When Jesus came into the coasts of Caesarea Philippi, he asked his disciples, saying, "Whom do men say that I the Son of man am?" And they said, "Some *say that thou art* John the Baptist; some, Elias; and others, Jeremias, or one of the prophets."
> —*Matthew 16:13–14 (KJV)*

Names are so important, and for me, choosing a title for a book is much like a proud papa finding just the right name to call his firstborn. You would not believe the struggle I had to name the baby now in your hands! Some of the material for this book emerged from a sermon series I preached entitled "Positioning Yourself for Prosperity." Naturally, I thought that a similar title might work well for the material and life lessons I wanted to share in this book. However, I quickly realized how emotionally, socially, and politically charged a term like *prosperity,* or the "P-word," as I like to call it, can be.

So as you can see, I found a title that seems more accurate to me and conveys a clearer sense of where I'm coming from. I didn't mind eliminating the P-word and all its connotations, denotations, and detonations from the title! In part, because I didn't want to risk being positioned in a camp of preachers who some say have marginalized the Gospel and relegated it in favor of capitalist ideals.

These speakers, preachers, and movements have been labeled, and many of them even embrace the way others perceive them. And it isn't hard to be labeled. Most of us are labeled by someone who, for example, studied us through a TV series we spoke on while they were doing their research. Some only base their label on one sermon or a night they were flicking through the TV channels and heard us say something that they now use as a tagline to define us.

Christ Himself wasn't exempt from being mislabeled, as the text I selected to open this chapter illustrates. I am amazed to realize that He had to live with the assumptions that others had about who He was. His disciples informed Him who and what "some say" concerning Him. Like Jesus, you will learn, as I have, that your critics and even your garden-variety commentators do not always agree on who you are or what you are truly about. This is largely because their assessment is almost always based on what someone else said or what they read or an isolated incident that they heard about you. Getting to know people takes time (ask anyone who's ever been married!) and most people prefer short easy sound bites to the hard work of getting to know people firsthand.

Believe me, I know about labels—I've had more slapped on me than a package mailed from China! I have been called everything from "the next Billy Graham" to "the next Jesse Jackson"—now there's a contrast for you! Praised by some, I've had my life threatened by others for allowing the then vice president to speak at our church dedication service because in their view a man of God should not have allowed someone so liberal to speak. Later I was singed by those who thought I should ignore President Bush's invitations to the White House, originally because some felt he was too conservative. Later he faced mounting criticism regarding the war in Iraq and the botched response to Katrina.

Please allow me to make something clear about my actions. As a man of God, I hate war. And I was horrified, and openly said so, about the handling of Katrina. However, as a man of God, I must do more than protest—given a chance to do so, I must also facilitate meaningful dialogue between opposing views for the betterment of all. To become totally identified with either side is not a luxury I believe we can afford when both major political parties will have long tenures of power when elected. In a crisis, actions outweigh anger, and often we must lay aside our frustrations and work to get our neighbors off the roof and out of the water rather than screaming at cameras for more to be done.

Being caught in between such polarizations isn't a new phenomenon, nor is it exclusively my plight. In your own life, you must live with the constant criticisms of opposing views, especially if you try to build fraternity between disparate sides and do as Christ said and be a peacemaker. Even if you choose a side based on a strong conviction you hold, you'll find those within the same group do not all share that view. Trust me, all Baptists do not agree! All megachurches are not monolithic and full of cookie-cutter types of people. Just because people share some common elements does not mean that they are suddenly identical in their views, beliefs, methods, and motives.

Such generalizations create the foundation for stereotypes, bias, and prejudice. This is why labels can be so detrimental to you as you progress in your success, and why it can be even harder to avoid the many labels that will be placed on you. A label, even one connoting success, doesn't have to be something that you put on yourself. People will gladly label you to suggest that you are one of them or to give themselves a foothold when they are coming in for the kill!

Add to that the deluge of labels that carry so much baggage in a simple word or phrase—*evangelical, charismatic, Pentecostal, conservative, moderate, feminist,* and, yes, even "prosperity preacher"—and you begin to see how many different things "some say" that I am. No doubt, you have been through this in your own life in one way or another. But you must keep in mind that as long as you know who you are, you can't always control what "some say" about you.

Peeling Off the Label of Prosperity

Since ultimately I can't control who wants to brand me as a professor of the P-word, I've learned to sidestep the whole question as an obstruction to my goals. The primary reason that this highly charged label does not bother me is that there is no such thing as the so-called prosperity gospel. First, the path to prosperity is not a straight line mapped on a graph by a motivational guru, business tycoon, or life coach, despite what the self-help section of the bookstore might have us believe. And second, I believe the word *gospel* in the context of faith has only one meaning. To the Christian, there is only one Gospel: God's grace extended through the death, burial, and resurrection of our Lord. We must never confuse the benefits with the payday. God offers us eternal life, not everlasting use of a Rolls-Royce!

You see, prosperity cannot be a gospel unto itself. It has no bible, no orthodox ideals that teach a definitive way to reach its capitalistic, tax-sheltered heaven. No, there is no prosperity gospel. Many who have been labeled "prosperity preachers" have been unfairly labeled, and their true message has been oversimplified by extremists who teach without balance and by alarmists who sensationalize without support. As in my case, one or two comments out of thirty years of ministry doesn't make me a prosperity preacher—no more than cooking a hamburger makes me a chef!

Those who have really followed my ministry down through the years know that my focus has always been on helping hurting people through messages like *Woman, Thou Art Loosed!* and others. Admittedly, I have written and sold a lot of books, invested wisely, bought and sold countless properties, written and produced music, plays, and movies, and I have prospered. But there is no magic to my method, just a lot of hard work and God's grace over what I authored and where I invested my time and resources. In ministry I have consistently tried to encourage and lift up people who were emotionally, socially, or sexually abused. Only a very small percentage of my teaching ministry focuses on finances. When I do bring them up, it's generally to say to people that if God blessed me with skills and resources, however limited the former and small the latter, then He can help anyone—from ex-cons to executives—build and shape their lives.

I'm convinced that those who focus on giving as the only or primary mechanism of economic empowerment teach people a magic that will lead only to frustration and disappointment. Trust me, the road up from poverty is not easy. One must know that one is gifted by God to succeed over adversity and injustice. It requires more than faith—though faith sure helps. But faith works only when you work it. It isn't enough to believe it; you must also give it life by working toward what you believe.

Hard work, relentless commitment, debt reduction, small investments, home ownership, and education are the tools that will help create long-term-stable financial health. I believe what Psalms 1 says about those who are blessed: "Whatsoever he doeth shall prosper." God not only blesses us when we give to charities and causes that are of interest to Him. He also blesses us when we have plans that line up with His purpose for our lives. Philanthropy may be of help to people and causes, it may even provoke blessings, but long-term prosperity requires more than passive faith and a lifetime of waiting. Productivity is required.

There's no one certain method to reach the goals of prosperity. Oprah got there one way. Diddy got there another. Bill Gates came another way. Condoleezza Rice arrived by a more academic route. From Tony Robbins to Baskin-Robbins, who can assure you of a one-way formula? All distinctly different: none has a methodology guaranteeing that the same formula will work for you.

Each route to a balanced, prosperous life is just as individual and unique as the person who is taking the journey. For you see, true prosperity doesn't come from the outside. It comes from within. It isn't just about money; it is about a relentless commitment to progress. Prosperity is more about having a balanced and centered life without losing control of what God has given you. In Christian lingo, this is stewardship. Personal responsibility falls within the same purview as fulfilling our God-given potential.

No matter what we call it, the process of embracing the fulfillment of our potential often creates a complex set of challenges with those around us. They will work hard to reduce the complexity and uniqueness of our hard work to a handful of clichés, adjectives, and labels. Can this be avoided? Not in my experience or from what I've observed and discussed with hundreds of other successful individuals from diverse backgrounds. Can it be minimized and managed so that it will not impede your ascent and abet the other obstacles brought on by your success? Absolutely!

Managing the Message

My friend John Maxwell teaches that the purest definition of leadership is influence. If that's true, then progressive prosperity will bring increased influence along with it. Influence is always monitored by those around you, and typically it serves as the fuel for your power base. It's very difficult to have it and not use it. And if you use it and others see it, they will always try to determine how they can garner it, draw from it, capitalize on it, or if all else fails, destroy it.

If you have it, someone will see it. If you have it on the job, someone will try to harness it and use it. If you have it with the boss, someone will try to deliver their message through your mouth. The most difficult part of the stewardship of success isn't getting the influence but maintaining the influence without it becoming contaminated by those who seek to use that which you have been blessed to attain.

If you are not watchful, you will find that those with whom you associate or even those who start to associate with you for their own motives will try to co-opt your talents. Regardless of which group it is, you can easily become a dummy. No, I am not name-calling—I mean a dummy literally. You know, the kind that sits on the lap of a ventriloquist and the dummy's mouth moves but it's the ventriloquist who's actually doing the talking. Is someone else's voice coming through your mouth when your lips move? Most of us don't relish the thought of being used so completely by someone else, but as we become more and more successful, the risk of others speaking for us only increases.

So think about it: Who speaks for you? This is one question that must be answered. And another of equal importance is Who speaks *to* you? Whoever speaks to you and speaks for you can be a very helpful or a major destructive force in your life. The person who speaks for you may often have an agenda that makes them attracted to the job of speaking for you. They need to borrow your influence to get their own messages delivered and their own private agenda accomplished.

All of us have people who speak for us. The mother who has a child answering the phone or carrying a message to the teacher has someone speaking for her. Your secretary or personal assistant may draft memos or letters for you based on her understanding of a certain conversation or phone call. Often those of us in business have midlevel management teams that convey the messages from the boardroom down to the staff and individual team members who need to be informed or who will execute the action points. Inevitably, such people end up speaking for you.

Have you noticed the press person who speaks for the president? I was always impressed by Ari Fleischer, who handled the press during the first term of the Bush administration. Or President Clinton's press secretary, Dee Dee Myers, fielding myriad questions from a variety of journalists. Can you imagine the weight of that job? Who would want to be responsible for misquoting the highest office in the nation? We do not have the influence that the president has, but in our own worlds, we are the president in some way. Who is your spokesperson and how much can you trust them with the stewardship of your message points?

I personally know what it is like to have to live with the consequences of someone who speaks for you. I have done interviews and walked away feeling great about my effectiveness only to find out the next morning that the reporter either knowingly or unknowingly misquoted me, or more often than not used the interview as a chance to get his or her opinions out through my story!

I've almost choked on my coffee more than once as I read something in the paper that I was supposed to have said but didn't. There someone was positioning me where and how they wanted for whatever purpose they deemed necessary, and suddenly I had lost stewardship of my own message points. Reporters themselves may not be newsworthy. But they can still speak through your interview simply by the way they arrange the facts. A few facts that are used and a few that are ignored, and there are you a year later trying to clean up the mess left behind by those who have misrepresented you.

Let me use a more common example. Have you ever had someone prepare your tax returns? If so, they were speaking for you. Have you ever hired an attorney to look into something for you or represent you in some legal matter? Have you ever hired a real-estate agent to sell or buy a property on your behalf? If so, these people were speaking for you. To the degree of their competence and integrity, you have success or failure.

To those of you who own a business, I want to give you something to think about. One of the hardest things to acquire is not financing or advertising or even facilities. It is quality people who will not misrepresent you. It doesn't matter what type of business you are in; if it grows, you will need staff to help you. The challenge is to find competent people who represent you well. Often the vision in the office is lost in the warehouse!

Somewhere between the conception of the idea, the development of the plan, and its implementation, the personality and attitude of the owner is diluted or polluted by those who handle the execution of the plan. In fact, in many cases, these handlers don't execute it, they outright kill it! Many great ideas, great churches, and great companies fail because of the disconnect between the visionary and those who represent her.

Overnight Delivery

What do you do when you want a package sent quickly and don't want it delayed by countless handlers and carriers? When that's the case, you pay a little extra and send it for overnight delivery. Similarly, when people want things done quickly, they often use your influence to deliver their message in a way that they perceive as being more expeditious. Most of us do it innocently enough.

A mother may say to her children, "Your father said that it's time for you to go to bed!" She uses his role and invokes his authority to convey her message. Or perhaps in some homes it is the reverse. "Your mother is going to be really upset if you don't unload the dishwasher!" Such phrases are as common as a cold in December. They are the ways in which others steer issues to conclusion when they need to borrow your influence.

Now, these domestic examples I cite are generally harmless enough. They are often expressions of your influence over this person or set of circumstances in which your name is invoked like magic and stated like a password. But not all cases are as innocent as a weary parent trying to elicit a positive response from a disgruntled child. There is always the person at work who uses your name in order to get a project done. Like saying "Open sesame!," using the name of someone who has influence opens doors and gains access. "I'm with the senator's office" can come from the mouth of an official spokesperson as well as from the janitor! In most of my organizations, one of the challenges I have historically faced is the propensity people have to use my name as a way to achieve their own wishes. While many of my staff are empowered to use my name and therefore my authority to accomplish my goals through them, sometimes they succumb to the temptation to use my name to fulfill their own agenda, not mine.

In fact, some people will often position themselves around you just to gain the influence such an association provides. It is amazing how people will try to ride in your car when they know it is going somewhere! Often I have found you don't even have a chance to speak their name, so busy are they dropping yours like fairytale children drop bread crumbs in a forest. They use it as a way of saying to people, "See, I am important!" or "Do you know who I know?"

What can you do when you have built integrity behind your name but others with less integrity hook up with you like a trailer hitch on the back of a car and go along for the ride? Unfortunately, sometimes there's not much! I have learned that this name-it-and-claim-it approach to influence often goes on while you are not even there to protest.

However, you must try to keep others' overnight deliveries to a minimum. If you are to avoid and manage the labels that others put on you, you must be aware of who is using your name and message for their own agenda. Your name and reputation quickly become diluted and your message corrupted when these power players usurp your identity.

Inserts and Flyers

You must also realize that a person doesn't have to be authorized to speak for you in order to assume that he can do so. I have been amazed at how many people start speaking for you just because you have been seen with them. These persons may only know you casually and like to project to others the idea that they know you better than they do. And I must warn you: Perception is almost as powerful as truth in the minds of many people. That is why whom you are seen with is a really important issue for the way you position and reposition yourself for success.

Believe it or not, you inadvertently give a certain amount of power to people just by being seen with them. Often you are held to be guilty by association. If you're seen with a member of either political party, suddenly it's assumed by the public that you support their party's entire agenda! Or if you attend an event where a certain celebrity is present, the media may imply that you condone the celebrity's fast-paced lifestyle. This is a word to the wise to choose carefully those with whom you are associated. The person with whom you interact may often use that relationship, consciously or unconsciously, to increase his own sphere of influence. It's like trickle-down economics—the influence keeps trickling down until there's very little of your original power and influence left.

Other associates may get close enough to you only to use you as a representative of the opposition to their view on a given issue. After mingling with you, they move back into their world and give their opinion, and suddenly you are considered to be despicable because you dare to disagree with them. Some people will even judge and condemn you just by observing whom you are with and inferring the nature of the relationship. And, unfortunately, often their conclusion is not flattering.

In such cases, relationships are like inserts and flyers. They are attached to something you do want, such as a newspaper, magazine, or personal mail, because typically you wouldn't look at the ads if they arrived alone.

Or think about those aggravating little advertising pop-ups that invade your computer screen like secret agents scurrying through a foreign country? Perhaps you logged on to get a wristwatch and there you are confronted by a pop-up advertisement for Viagra! Or vice versa!

Just because they are extremely aggravating doesn't mean that they aren't effective. If they weren't effective, companies wouldn't use them. According to America Online, one of the largest consumer internet service providers, the number of pop-up advertisements totals around five billion for each quarter—that's potentially twenty billion interruptions a year!

Similarly, some people work hard to insert themselves into areas of your life where they try to siphon off your energy, attention, and influence. These pop-up personalities just show up on your stage, in your life, at your house, not because they earnestly want a relationship, but because they need to borrow your influence.

The next thing you know, you're in association with someone or something largely because you are being blessed in some way unrelated to them, and they want to go along for the ride. But that is not the worst part. The worst part is the baggage that they bring along and the way it places you in a precarious situation whereby you often inherit their enemies simply by your silence. Suddenly you learn things about yourself that have very little or no basis in the reality of the relationship, situation, or circumstance.

Mailing Labels

The first time I learned I had "the ear" of the president and served as his spiritual adviser was when I read about it in the paper. In no time at all, I was getting calls from every Tom, Dick, or Mary who wanted me to give the president some vital message. It took me a while to realize that people actually thought that he and I were going to Wendy's to get a big one with cheese!

I was astonished that a couple of luncheons which were exactly the same ones I attended under other administrations had now been "spinned" into stories about the two of us good old boys hanging out at the country club, hitting golf balls at a resort, and sailing on a yacht! It was hilarious! In reality, he was governor when I came to Texas, I met him at a luncheon, and I knew him as well as you know anyone with whom you ate with once and sat beside during a couple of meetings.

Not that being close to President Bush or any political figure is a bad thing. I have always thought it was an honor to be invited to attend any event held by presidents from either party. But people don't seem to realize that having lunch with any of them does not mean that I agree or disagree with their policies. However, it might give me a chance to mention my perspectives, and for that I am grateful. I have and will continue to try to influence and to gain information that I can communicate back into our communities and help our people. I believe that in order to effect change you must sometimes work from the outside by sharing ideas for serious consideration.

When the media take on an issue or print a story, they don't often ask you what is fact and what is perception. They just write it, meet the deadline, and go on to the next story! I look around at the media and the national attention being given to the immigration issue, for example, and suddenly hundreds of Hispanic pastors are ready to picket my church because they think I have the power to persuade the president to give all immigrants green cards. This is happening all the while I am trying to get a parking ticket reduced (unsuccessfully, I might add) at the county office! How can someone with modest political influence at best be perceived to influence the leader of the free world? A simple, one-word powder keg: *labels*.

In your own life, it might not be what is printed about you. It may be what is perceived about you. But I want to warn you that perception and reality are not the same thing. All of us have had people who said things about us that were only partially or sometimes not at all accurate. From our schoolyard days of "she thinks she's something" to the office watercooler gossip—"Did you hear that they hooked up?"—we are all trying to live with labels and perceptions that people often use and have without accurate facts.

Like the stamp of "priority mail" or "first class" on a parcel-post package, labels are what people use to categorize you for easy handling. They put you in a group. "Is he the next Billy Graham?" "She reminds me of a young Oprah." "He's a little like Denzel." On and on and on, all of these labels help people to describe you. But they rob you of your God-given uniqueness and cause you often to be misfiled for years, and all because people are making assumptions based on associations!

When such labels continue to get applied and passed along, when the package keeps getting tossed and shipped between its starting point and its destination, they quickly lead to bias and prejudice. Racism, sexism—choose your stereotype and then begin peeling away the layers. The package you find beneath those many stamps and stickers may be very different from the one you saw when it first appeared.

All of us are living with labels that may not describe who we are but provoke an image we have to live with. From evangelicals to gay rights activists, no group is reducible to a simple term. But for the person who paints with broad strokes it is easy to label and move on. Racial, social, sexual, and political labels are just as inaccurate a way of describing a person as a zip code assures you that a person has good or bad credit! Yet many of us are treated unfairly simply because we are around others who feel or think a certain way. If you are to arrive at your destination on time, then you must make sure that the proper mailing label is the one that others see first.

Handlers and Carriers

As you become more successful, one of the limitations that you must contend with, one that may be more prevalent and complicated because you have gained stature, wealth, and visibility from your growing success, is the effect of the labels others will stick on you. Certainly you must do all you can to stay in control of your name, your reputation, and what is said about you. You must be diligent about making sure that your messages and missions are not miscommunicated or misrepresented.

However, you are only one person, and the more successful you become, the more you will be forced to rely on others to sustain your success and move you forward. You may need accountants, lawyers, coworkers, shippers, decorators, caterers, and others to help you execute your various goals. You simply cannot do it all without others whom you trust and rely on. So how do you discern the method you need to employ in order to avoid the snares of false perceptions and inaccurate labels?

As I close this chapter, I want to define two groups of people: handlers and carriers. Some people are like mail handlers. They handle you out of necessity and sometimes out of their own need for association. Inevitably we are all being handled every day. But if you have more people handling you than you do carrying you, then you will end up fondled but not forwarded!

Handlers touch, hold, and hassle. Carriers move with your momentum. I challenge you to surround yourself with people who can carry you and manage those who handle you. Do not allow others to control you and hijack your mission. You must remember that your lawyer doesn't make the decisions for you; he is simply provided with the information and describes your options. He may advise or recommend, but he doesn't decide. You are the only one who can decide!

Don't allow the people around you to run you. It is so easy to do. I have done it myself and had to live with the consequences of their decisions, lack of wisdom, lack of understanding of my vision, or just plain old manipulation. The goal is to gather a strong team of people around you who perform with excellence but don't try to coach the team. You must call the plays. They carry the mail, but they don't write it! Write your own mail, choose your own destination, and in so doing, you can reposition yourself rather than allowing others to reposition you and send you to the dead-letter office!

Don't be surprised or fooled by the challenges that will come from your ongoing success. Others will try to jump in and steal little bits and pieces of who you are or turn you into what they want you to be. Some will handle you to death, absorbing all they can from the contact. But others will carry you, move you forward, empower and encourage you to remain true to who you are and what you're about. Surround yourself with these carriers and serve others in the same capacity as opportunities allow.

Keep your momentum flowing as you're growing, never slowing!

fourteen
Flight Manual—Soaring and Landing with Success at Home

And when Jesus came to the place, he looked up, and saw him, and said unto him, Zacchaeus, make haste, and come down; for to day I must abide at thy house.
—*Luke 19:5 (KJV)*

As I shared in the introduction to this third section, part of my inspiration for writing this book emerged from an awareness that Zacchaeus had the forethought and tenacity to run ahead of others and to climb a tree, thereby repositioning himself for what Jesus would do next. While he's clearly someone who desired more, who had to reposition himself beyond the limits of his own success, I believe that the key to understanding his story emerges in the surprising message he receives from Jesus.

When the Lord says to the publican, "I must abide at thy house," He throws a stone into the calm, in-control surface of Zacchaeus's little pond. He makes it clear that He's not just delivering a drive-by blessing on His way to some other event. He plans to stop and get to know this strange little man who's willing to climb a tree to catch a glimpse of Him.

In His response to Zacchaeus, Christ reinforces the concept of integration that we so admired earlier in the Proverbs 31 woman. This integrated, holistic perspective on success begs us to ask the hard questions. *What good are fame and fortune if our hearts are mired by famine and fatigue? What good is what we capture at the marketplace if it doesn't translate into what we carry back into our place of abode!* Progress isn't progress if it diminishes the place we live and who we really are as a people.

Could it be that we can use this story somewhat metaphorically to bring Christ from the public places of our own lives into the intimate living space of the converted soul? Could it be that bankruptcy is replaced by wealth when the spirit of Christ permeates our dwellings?

Home Work

Let me submit that true faith is not attained until that encounter with God invades your personal space, your heart, and your home. The hardest thing for many of us to do is to reconcile who we are publicly with who we are privately. It is almost like we all have a set of twins inside of us, but they are not identical at all. These twins are extremely different yet share the same space like fraternal twins do. One of them is our ideal self, the person we want to be and we want all who know us to believe that we are. But then there is the real self, who may be less polished, may be limited, and may lack the skills to navigate an effective relationship. The real person may have blemishes that we try fiercely to keep from view. Like Jacob and Esau in the Bible who fought each other, our twins may be in conflict. These two "selves" often wrestle for control, fighting—no, warring—one against the other until we are miserable, along with those who want to love us, from the constant battle we are waging inside.

Too many times the attempt to live up to our ideal selves depletes us and causes discontentment with our real selves. This dissonance is the inner turmoil we struggle with daily, often, most notably, at home. This takes domestic disputes to a whole new level!

And the reality is this: Whatever we feed is what we grow. If we feed the home life, it will grow stronger. If we feed the work life, it will grow stronger. But what do you do when you need both? Eventually you may achieve a successful career, but a faltering home life means that it is all for naught. Or you can have a great home life, but if someone doesn't provide more than love, then dinner isn't very romantic when all you can order is water!

The only viable solution is the hard-to-attain balance that gives us a well-rounded, satisfying life. But it's challenging to channel our attention and effort, in a balanced way, into the many needs and demands that require our attention. We easily drift to extremes rather than maintain our equilibrium and dwell in the center of who we really are and want to be.

Generally, most of us have a propensity to focus more completely on gaining *for* home rather than gaining *at* home. Could it be possible that sometimes what it takes to make us successful in public is counterproductive to a strong home life? Most successful people are not the ones who are home by five o'clock or the ones who take long, luxurious vacations with their families on private tropical islands. They are usually the ones who work well past dinnertime to pay for the lifestyle their families may have come to take for granted. On the other hand, many of the soccer moms that I see out there look blissfully happy, but budget-conscious.

Let's face it, those who get ahead in our society often do so at great cost to their family life and personal time of renewal. Consequently, it's not uncommon to see those who sit behind corporate desks, run for political office, manage banks, or even pastor churches sitting in divorce court with sealed documents, trying to manage a private failure gone public.

You may recall the mock intervention from our first chapter. In it, I wrote about a character named L Lover, who confronts the reader about his or her apathetical attitude about relationships. It is easy to slip into harboring feelings of detachment from and disinterest in others, and to wrongly assume that we have hidden them from others. It is expensive to invest our emotional assets in one person without going bankrupt in other emotional connections, especially when one has been drawn to love a needy person.

Often our bankruptcy isn't caused by a lack of interest in relationships but by the struggle to budget our emotional resources while simultaneously trying to fuel a successful business future. Many men and now women seem to think that providing financially is a replacement for providing attention and a sense of "thereness." Maintaining the house requires not only time but "presence" of mind. You can be physically home and emotionally a thousand miles away! I know what you are feeling and I have been there. Sometimes those of us who love what we do at work often feel that there isn't enough of us to go around for those we love at home.

The reality is that most of us lack the balance that it takes to be totally effective in both our business and private lives. Since success often requires sacrifice, something always goes lacking, and for many people it is time enjoying their families or just relaxing without being plugged into their "CrackBerry." For example, 24 percent of U.S. workers said they spend fifty or more hours on the job each week, with 22 percent claiming they work six to seven days a week. According to CNN, U.S. workers may be neglecting their health, personal relationships, and the quality of their work because of longer work hours and more stress on the job.

Since true prosperity doesn't mean swapping private success for public success but rather balancing them, it is imperative that you and I spend a little time discussing how we can better enhance our home lives. Most corporations are learning the hard way that an unhappy home life might be of little consequence initially in the workplace, but eventually those who are miserable at home become less productive at work. In fact, researchers report that stress caused by an imbalance between home and work costs our society $100 billion per year. Individuals who struggle with marital dysfunction, child-rearing issues, and personal adjustment transitions tend to be less productive at work, take more sick leaves, and have more conflict with coworkers.

So if success is going to last beyond the initial burst of commitment and short-range results, we have to figure a way to gain publicly without losing privately. And while this is not always easy, achieving it is always intentional. No one succeeds in both areas by accident. If we do not aim at it, constantly repositioning ourselves to attain it, we will build and buy houses but lose our homes. If we are not intentional about this, we will establish the highest credit rating just in time to start paying out child support.

As you progress in your success, it is very important that you bring your family with you. I have counseled dozens of families who grew, but in the process they often ended up growing apart. In the past ten years, over ten million divorces were granted in the United States. Think about this staggering statistic. According to the U.S. Census Bureau, the number of children living with a single parent rose by more than 200 percent from 1960 to 2000. Of those children, roughly 75 percent live with the mother (U.S. Census Bureau, 2000, "Living Arrangements of Children Under 18 Years Old: 1960 to Present," available online at www.census.gov/population/socdemo/hh-am/tabCH-1.txt). Married couples who drift apart emotionally often end up separating physically.

How can you avoid becoming part of these disheartening statistics as you become more successful? I believe you must pay attention not only to the kind of takeoff you want to make, but to the kind of landing you want to make as well. No matter how successful you are, you'll never enjoy the ride to the fullest without having those you love by your side and without preparing a soft place for you to land.

The Launching Stage

In 1903, American aeronautical engineers Orville and Wilbur Wright built the first working airplane. At Kitty Hawk, North Carolina, on December 17, 1903, Orville Wright made the first successful flight of a piloted, heavier-than-air, self-propelled craft, called the Flyer, traveling a distance of about 120 feet.

We have come a long way since then, but attaining great heights still requires a launching place and the space in which to soar. A new 747 has tremendous thrust and power. It can fly easily at forty thousand feet. It holds hundreds of people and cargo and yet can defy the laws of gravity and lift its weight and thousands of additional pounds to heights that would once have been beyond human comprehension. However, in spite of its size and thrust, wing power and design, it cannot get off the ground without ample run-ways. In order for it to overcome the laws of gravity and become airborne, it has to taxi down the runway and gain momentum.

People are no different really. We often have to "fly" through turbulent situations, from office politics to unfair treatment based on bias and prejudice. We have to overcome limited finances, the scoffing of our families at our dreams, and much more if we are to produce a level of prosperity that impacts the next generation. More times than not, those who love us become more than the crew and attendants. They literally become the launching place through whom we are able to taxi up on success and stretch our ambitious wings to see new horizons materialize.

The launching stage, as I like to call it, is the stage when the whole family has one vision and goal. Each has a role to play and all feel connected to the dream. Just as certainly as Joseph's dream affected his brothers, most of us are forced to include the whole family in the dream we have in order to get the support base we need to realize it. This means that all of those around us need to "buy into" the dream in order to bring it to fruition. In the early stages of success, the whole family generally participates in the process. Dad goes back to school for night classes, mom takes on an extra job, and the kids know to keep quiet while he is studying. They all work together to get the job done. They all share in the degree when their combined hard work comes to fruition.

I have a friend whose mother went back to school to be a nurse. The whole family was helping her, reviewing homework, asking questions to ensure she had mastered her lecture notes, assisting in the acquisition of needed materials for extra credit on homework. Home-cooked meals turned into fast food and pot pies. *Laundry* ended up becoming an archaic term for which few could find a def-inition. The normal routine of the family was altered drastically.

By the time their mother had accomplished the task, the whole house knew something about medicine and was a lot more educated as a result of one of them going after her dream. They also wore a lot of wrinkled clothing. They were the runway she ran down as she gained the velocity needed to fly to her dream. Though it requires sacrifice, an intangible cost that cannot be measured by tuition dollars and charges in the university bookstore, most people will pay their share when they love you and care about your dreams.

And I have heard countless stories of upwardly mobile people whose families, either the immediate ones or broader family networks, make a concerted effort so that one of them had opportunities that the others might not have. I have a dear friend whose wife worked like a dog while he went to school. It often takes the unified effort of everyone around you to revive a family whose circumstances have become dismal.

The process is comparable to an obese person deciding he is going to lose weight. It often becomes difficult to impossible without the support of the family whose members (whether they need it or not) have to submit to low-caloric emphasis to assist the one person in achieving his goal. It is hard to accomplish a great feat without great support. This is so whether the person decides to go back to school, goes after a real-estate license, pursues a CPA, or whatever.

But once this stage is over, it is easy to live in two different realities. There is one reality at work and then there is the other one at home. *The real challenge for people is not to grow apart.* This isn't about falling apart. Growing apart is quiet and silent. It leaves no witness and it has no due date. No one can pinpoint when it happens. It is as quiet as the erosion of a riverbank and as lethal as the poisoning of a human system with strychnine. No one hears poison, but they can see its effects. So it is in the growing apart of a household.

One gentleman shared with me how embarrassed he was to bring his wife to company outings. She knew nothing about contemporary politics and seemed bored by the schmoozing that went on at the events his new job required him to attend. His wife felt embarrassed and uncomfortable with the women whose lives read like the society pages, while she was interested in the latest PTA issues. He was embarrassed and their home was falling apart because he, and these are his words, "had outgrown his wife." What made this a painful separation was that she had worked while he went to school, going without things she wanted because she believed in his dream. But once the dream was achieved, it drove them apart rather than binding them together.

I know you say love is enough to hold things together, but to paraphrase a line from a song in *Fiddler on the Roof*: A bird and a fish can fall in love, but if they do, where would they live? Often love is not enough when transitions occur and one of you doesn't move in the same direction as the other. And if you do not grow together, then you increase the very real risk of growing apart. It was almost as if the husband described above was punishing his wife for being loyal to his dream to the point of sacrificing her own development. But wait a minute before you nail him to the tree— feelings of guilt do not make a relationship last. Anyone can feel benevolence. Yet no one wants to be loved as a charity. We must grow together in love if we are to share the dream and sustain it. Since achieving a dream takes time, we must learn how to support each other consistently, particularly during the stalls and delays that we're bound to face.

The Layover Stage

All of us from time to time find ourselves in need of a pit stop, oil change, or whatever it takes to recalibrate and refuel. And the point where we know we need it, but also know we are not yet able to make it happen, is often where we find ourselves feeling discouraged and stuck.

When the children of Israel left for the Promised Land, they did so because Moses had described to them a land that flowed with milk and honey. However, he didn't mention that they would spend years getting there. Most meaningful progress comes in stages or phases. It takes great faith to endure the phases that don't seem to be as comfortable or as rewarding as the ultimate destination. Oddly enough, I have come to realize that the destination is not the place where growth is attained and learning is a process, not a product. We learn everything from planning to be patient in between destinations.

Sometimes we come to the layover stage in God's design, and sometimes we end up there because one of us is simply too tired to maintain the pace and passion of success! It is easier for the one in the light to be excited. Far easier for them than for the one who is carrying the lamp oil. Often we handle these stages differently depending on whether the vision was as important to one as it was to the other member of a couple. Often people who love you go along for the ride, but that doesn't mean that they have bought into the destination. Sometimes they are just going because it is your direction.

They eventually get weary with the demands and need to refuel. They are not as charged by the destination as you are. It is here where more transparent questions and conversation ensues. It is difficult when what fuels one of you is draining the other one. Often it happens in such a way that the one who is being fueled is oblivious to the fact that the other is being drained. Many people get divorced or go for family counseling in total shock. They never even knew there was a problem! However, later, in retrospect, they can see the telltale signs that something was awry.

In-Flight Success

If you are to succeed without losing the people who are most important to you along the way, then here are a few suggestions. Knowing these tips may keep you from gaining on one end only to lose on the other.

1. **Introduce your flight crew**

   Have you ever noticed how a truly great performer always introduces the band? Similarly, when you first board a plane, the crew chief usually introduces all who will be serving you on board. As the pilot of your ascending success, it should be your responsibility to help create an atmosphere for the people you love to dwell in. This is especially vital with upwardly mobile women whose work life has taken you someplace where your husband feels out of place. It can be a very uncomfortable struggle for a man who is holding the arm of a woman who is chairman of the board while he scoops ice cream for a living. There's nothing wrong with scooping ice cream, of course, and it only becomes a problem when others begin comparing the husband to other men in the room.

   I recommend being preemptive: Before anyone gets a chance to evaluate your spouse, tell your coworkers the story of how this person has supported you along the way. Explain that you are who you are today because of their support and love. This way you can turn misery into victory by introducing the band.

2. Bring the people you love with you

You always have a choice to bring them or leave them. Including them in conversations at home helps them to feel connected to your world and gives them some sense of what it is like to be you. It also helps them to understand your stress points and what is going on at work that might have you disconnected at home or troubled in some way. They don't have to become an expert to gain enough basic information to steer through a conversation and not feel intimidated by your newfound success level and the people by whom you are now surrounded.

3. Keep the main thing the main thing

It is very easy to turn your family, who once served as your supporting cast and provided for you while you were launching, into extras. They become extras on your new set, fillers performing for your enhancement, losing all sense of personhood, nameless faces in your production. How do you prevent them from fading into the background of your life while you ascend to new heights? It's easy to talk about keeping our priorities straight, but how do we keep the main thing truly our main thing?

Do you remember the movie *The Matrix*? The intriguing thing about this film was the difficult task of determining which world was the actual and which was the Matrix. In this fascinating story of technology gone awry, the Matrix becomes the simulated world that fools the characters into believing it is real. As pawns in this cyber-driven power struggle, humans exist in tiny pods and have no "real" life.

Unfortunately, this can become a prophetic allegory of the life that awaits you when you become more successful. Sometimes if you are not careful, you can allow the job, the ministry, or whatever your goal has been to become more important than the home, when in fact, it is home that you are working to build. Work is just the tool you are using to build it. You have a responsibility to keep the main thing the main thing.

This means that you have to establish continually that the world you have at work is not the real world for you but is only a matrix, which can enhance the real and more important world in which you live. This message has to be played and replayed in your own ears, lest the work life cannibalize your personal life until there is no home left. You'll wake up one day and find yourself in a house that lives and breathes to support a career that you will later learn is not enough to sustain a human existence. Build your home from the inside out, and remember why you're working long hours and whom you're doing it for. Don't allow the rush of the latest deal or the prospect of a new income-tax bracket to eclipse the constellation of familial stars shining around you.

4. Dignify others with your attention

Finally, invest some energy in the interests of the people in your home life. It humbles the soul and keeps you grounded, prevents you from becoming so myopic that you lose sight of the children's needs or your spouse's needs. It is hard not to love someone who is interested in us and what we do. If you are going to be married to someone who shovels trash, then learn something about receptacles, trucks, and back braces. Buy a brace every now and then and listen while they share what it is like for them to be them. People leave, if not physically then emotionally, when they feel you are out of touch with them and their reality. If you learn something more about them and they learn more about you, then you've grown toward each other by meeting in the middle.

Prepare for Landing

If you have flown very much, then you know how choppy the air can become as the plane descends from the smooth levels at thirty-six thousand feet. Winds and weather patterns can create enough bumps and jarring jolts to frighten even the most seasoned traveler. In our careers, there is usually quite a bit of turbulence in our landings as well as in our flights. In part, because the house has adjusted to your being distracted. In part, because you whose career or life is extremely exciting needs a level of fulfillment that seems impossible to obtain from the grandstand filled with only four people, some of whom are more interested in homework than in headlines, in school newsletters than in the *Wall Street Journal*.

You would be amazed at how many ministers have little to discuss with you once they run out of things to say about what they do every day. Like aging athletes going through withdrawal from the world of sports, any of us can find it rough landing back into normalcy. From playing in the Pro Bowl to cleaning the toilet bowl is quite a leap! After their flights to fame, they find themselves frustrated trying to align themselves with the runway that takes them home again.

Not that different are inmates freed from prison, excited about leaving the penal institution but wondering if they can adjust to life on the outside. The doors slam behind them with a thud, the world opens before them, and they step into an atmosphere that may be more frightening in some ways than the one they left behind. They ride home liberated but also anxious. Often they wake up in the middle of the night, tense and worried, reliving scenes and scenarios from the past, trying to adjust to a new set of expectations.

Anytime you have built your life outside of the house, coming home and being happy there can be a daunting task. You may have to work your way into a safe landing or you will crash and burn. Haven't you often wondered why so many marriages crash and burn after twenty years? The couple did excellently when the work was between them, the children were between them. But when the obstacles were all removed, they couldn't find a way to land the plane.

Every eagle lands sometimes. Sooner or later, even soaring wings will grow weary and the eagle will want to land. Here are a few tips to consider that might help you have a smooth landing.

Foremost, it's easier not to land all at once. You do not see planes come down like helicopters losing momentum too fast. Instead you will hear the pilot say, "Ladies and gentlemen, please fasten your seat belts as we prepare for our descent." Now, that is exactly what we must do: prepare for our descent rather than attempt a crash landing.

Preparing for a smooth descent requires several things. Is there a retirement plan in place? Where are you going to live and with whom? You can't wait until you're landing to think of these things. In order to ascertain what your retirement plans should be, you have to answer a series of questions that you may have been too busy to consider while you were in flight. It might be as simple as determining what lifestyle you need to shift into. What cities are best for retired persons? You don't have to be old to decide that you are ready to semiretire, slow down a little, start nesting more and enjoying what the work was all about. But if you have no plan, you have planned to fail! What is the cost of living in your area and at what rate is it escalating? How large will your pension be by the time you need to use it? All of this is something that can be computed. What you cannot compute is how you will cope with the normalcy and the absence of the high-stress life many of you have become addicted to while in the air.

Another major consideration of a practical nature: How do you fit back into the lives of the people who helped you fly? Are they not sometimes familiar strangers? Are you still needed? How do you regain a stable role in your own house? Is there anybody left to love, or have you had such profound losses in that area that the people you were doing it for are no longer there when you're ready to land? Will you have to divert your intended flight plan and reestablish new relationships?

Don't try to land too fast. Give people as much chance to adjust to your return as you did for them to adjust to your departure. Now that you are trying to regain entrance into the lives of those you love, don't expect your old role to have been left vacant all of these years while you were earning and learning and burning up the airways! They may have simply moved on in some ways that are bound to cause you distress merely because they are unfamiliar.

Now, don't do like the criminals do who go back to jail simply because they don't know how to fit back into their own world. You see, you can love the idea of something and not be able to handle its reality. Ex-prisoners love the idea of being freemen, but the reality is difficult for them. The businessman loves the idea of a family vacation. But he might find himself feeling like he has been harpooned into a National Lampoon vacation!

You Can Take It With You

Just remember that you must incorporate your family and loved ones into each and every stage of your life, whether it's ascending, leveling off, or descending. Learn to take the excitement of your career and public pursuits into your home and share it with those who are committed to you and your well-being. They want to be a part of whatever it is you are going through if you will only let them. Focus on relationships before market reports, time with the ones you love instead of time with ones you can barely tolerate!

Like the pilot who has trouble connecting the moving vehicle with the stable ground, you need direction from the control tower. I believe that God is in the tower to help you regain alignment so that you can assume some balance between the ideal you and the real you. He can assist you in finding a stable place to balance your turbocharged life. He can give you counsel as to how to fit into a world that you may have been disconnected to or been only mildly involved in.

This is why I believe that faith is so critical. Only God, who sits in the control tower, can show you how to realign what you did in the air with who you are at home. It is through His grace and direction that you will be positioned for a safe and satisfying landing. I am not speaking of dying here, just landing. Landing into the welcome arms of a life that is defined by more than what you have accomplished. I am talking about someone who waits for you and sees you as more than what fans or coworkers see. These are not colleagues who love you for what you do. These are people who value you for who you are. It is with them that you want to land. But you cannot land if you haven't any runway left to hold you as you come in for a landing.

What does it profit a man to gain this whole world and lose his soul? If you lose the core, what good are all the rest of your accomplishments? The love and shared moments are the only parts of you that you can truly take with you when you depart from this life and begin your final descent. You can't take your sports cars or your latest designer bling, your luxury condo in the islands or your portfolio. Only the things that matter most can accompany you on your next journey.

I challenge you to do what you must do today to reposition

your priorities and take your pursuit of success into your home. Remind the people in your life why you're doing what you do outside of the house by sharing your heart, your time, and your concerns with them. Let them in and keep them on board the flight with you. It will make your time in the air so much more meaningful and enjoyable and will guarantee a smooth landing in a destination that already feels like where you belong.

fifteen

Stay Connected— Utilizing Your Legacy to Build a Bridge

For the body is not one member, but many. If the foot shall say, Because I am not the hand, I am not of the body; is it therefore not of the body? And if the ear shall say, Because I am not the eye, I am not of the body; is it therefore not of the body? If the whole body *were* an eye, where *were* the hearing? If the whole *were* hearing, where *were* the smelling?

—*1 Corinthians 12:14–17 (KJV)*

One of my favorite short stories was written by Alice Walker, the Pulitzer Prize–winning author of *The Color Purple*. The story, called "Everyday Use," is about the relationship between a mother and her two grown daughters. They live in a rural area in the South, likely similar to the red-clay hills of North Georgia where the author grew up. The older daughter, the beautiful and stylish Dee, hates her impoverished, small-town upbringing and has made a new life for herself with a job, a car, and a boyfriend from the big city. Her younger sister, Maggie, the victim of serious burns from a childhood fire, still lives with their mother and approaches life cautiously. You've likely met women within the same family just like these, one of whom is larger than life, while the other seems to enjoy being a wallflower.

In this story, Dee comes home for a visit, the entitled princess returning to her roots to further reinforce how far she's come. While there, she asks her mother for quilts that had been hand-pieced by her namesake, Grandma Dee. The young woman explains that she wants to hang them as signs of her heritage. Suddenly the mother faces a real quandary, for she has promised the quilts to Maggie as part of her dowry when she marries her local beau. Dee is outraged and complains that her sister would be "backward enough to put them to everyday use," quickly reducing them to rags from the wear.

Maggie concedes the quilts, used to watching Dee get her way in life, and explains that she knows how to quilt and can make more. Their mother, however, in a kind of divine revelation, insists that these quilts belong to Maggie and offers Dee some other, machine-stitched versions. Dee leaves in a huff and Maggie and her mother enjoy a rare moment of satisfaction at the justice of the situation.

I love this story for many reasons, including the wonderful point it makes about the way that we often arrive at a certain level of success in life and then lose touch with the place from which we came. We suddenly think we're better than others because we moved out of the hood, got an education, and have a better job.

The story also reminds us to use what we have been given and what we've earned rather than trying to preserve them as museum pieces. We must seek to live out our heritage every day, enjoying the present moment as a precious legacy with which we have been entrusted through the sacrifices of our ancestors.

Roots and Branches

Another fine writer, Alex Haley, ushered in a phenomenal wave of interest in one's genealogy with his classic work *Roots*. As he examined the personal stories of his ancestors, he discovered common themes of endurance, sacrifice, hope, faith, and a deep abiding love that could not be contained by chains or diminished by segregation. New generations of Americans suddenly scurried to the library and the family Bible to piece together their own family trees, untangling the roots of stories every bit as compelling as Haley's.

Generally speaking, most African-Americans did not need to be reminded of the brutality, abuse, and prejudice that their forefathers and matriarchs endured. We have been very deliberate in preserving the family stories, orally told, along with artifacts such as letters, pictures, and other heirlooms. We value family and never want to lose sight of all that has been overcome in order for us to be positioned where we are presently.

However, as all of us of all ethnicities become more and more successful, the temptation to lose touch with the grounding of our roots—both historical and personal—looms before us. In some cases, a person simply becomes too busy, too addicted to the thrill of the next deal or the prospect of another promotion, to maintain contact with family members and traditions. Making sure everyone gets together for Christmas or a family reunion no longer seems like such a priority.

For others, who are beginning their path to fulfilling their dreams, it's not just a matter of busyness but of self-absorption. By this I mean that they no longer feel like they have anything in common with those who may have raised them, supported them, and applauded them as they excelled. Suddenly they are caught up in a corporate world of international conference calls, flights to meetings across the country, and twelve-hour workdays. Their corporate culture defines others by their educational degree, their designer suits, and their networking capabilities with other upwardly mobile professionals.

When this becomes the world in which you thrive, it can indeed become difficult to slip back into your overalls and head out to the country to enjoy Aunt Mabel's turnip greens and fatback. It can be challenging to return to the hood and experience painful memories of the less prosperous times from which you emerged. You may feel like you have changed in numerous ways, while your siblings, cousins, and childhood friends still seem exactly as they used to be.

The worst is when our extended families and childhood friends view us as having "sold out" because we have succeeded. Even if we don't feel superior to them, they think we do or being around us makes them feel "less than." They don't invite us to family get-togethers, or if they do, they make sure that we're treated like outcasts. This can be so painful because even though we are upwardly mobile, we're often not fitting in with the good old boys down at the country club or the ladies in the local Junior League. Recent statistics indicate the percentage of black families in the American middle class was one in ten in the 1960s and now, forty years later, it's one in three. We have indeed come a long way, baby, but with this upward mobility we often find ourselves isolated. We end up in a no-man's-land where it can be difficult to find anyone who relates and cares.

Family, however, often take their cues from us, and if we think that we're too high to stoop down to attend a family event, then we risk jeopardizing the very roots that now support our towering tree. It's one thing to become entangled in the roots of a tree and struggle to climb upward to higher branches. But it's another thing to get so high in the tree that you think you don't need the roots any longer and cut yourself off from them.

Much like Paul writing to the church at Corinth about interdependence rather than independence, we must learn that, like the foot and the hand, we are different in many ways but interconnected for the betterment of both. Often we lose sight of the connection that family provides and lead fragmented, out-of-touch lives of constant busyness. But this isn't good for the wholeness and congruence we all need to survive and thrive.

The metaphor may seem obvious to you, but if we are to grow, we must continue to receive the nourishment and support that roots provide for the rest of the branches. Maybe we find ways to show our families glimpses of the world we now live in so that they can better understand who we are and where we're headed. Perhaps we get honest with ourselves and realize that no matter how much our circumstances and résumés may have changed, there are aspects of us that remain the same. As we discussed earlier, someday our high-powered career will end and we'll be trying to land the plane of our success into retirement only to discover that there's no one waiting to greet us at the terminal.

How can you keep in touch with your roots even as you climb higher in the tree?

1. **Honor family traditions as much as possible.** To the extent that you are able, try to maintain the family traditions from your childhood. It may be inconvenient to attend Sunday din-

ner at Grandma's once a month, but you will cherish the time with her and other relatives once you're there. If you can afford to travel and visit family for important holidays and birthdays, then do it when your work and personal schedule allow. Find a balance between where you're going and where you've been.

2. **Be honest about the past without reliving it.** If it's painful to visit your parents because of what happened in the past. then be honest with yourself and them. Perhaps you need to take a sabbatical from family holidays for a few years while you get counseling and deal with your issues. Maybe you need to have a heart-to-heart conversation with a parent or relative who has hurt you. But whatever you do, don't allow yourself to continue reliving the incident; arguing, yelling, and crying will likely only keep your wound open.

3. **Create new traditions.** Whether with your immediate family or with your family of close friends, try to celebrate life in fresh, creative ways that contain no baggage from the past. Maybe it's how you celebrate birthdays with your girlfriends or how you and your children recognize the Sabbath as a day of rest. Maybe you've always wanted to have a Kwanzaa party or go dancing on Valentine's Day. Regardless of how you do it, find some ways to tailor such special occasions to your style and personality.

4. **Honor those who have contributed to your success.** Do you remember the words your grandmother shared with you on your wedding day? The prayer your father said before dinner each night? Perhaps it's time to have a calligrapher print such meaningful words on beautiful paper for framing. Or maybe it's placing the photo of your siblings in the kitchen where you'll see it every day. Maybe it's wearing your mother's pearls for the big presentation at work. Hold on to mementos of spe-

cial events when your family really supported you or encouraged your dream.

5. **Pass family stories along to your children.** It may be your own children, nieces and nephews, or young ones whom you are mentoring, but find a way to share stories of your family's past with the next generation. You may even want to write out stories that are especially moving, meaningful, or inspirational and give them as a gift to a child. Or maybe make a photo album or slide show. Remind them of what they're made of and the bond that exists within your family.

6. **Make family time sacred.** Whether you're married or single, your life will be enriched if you will find a consistent time to connect and really be present with your family. You need to do more than go through the motions with those you love. For your immediate family, it might be a special mealtime once a week (Mexican Mondays!) amid the flurry of busy schedules. For your extended family, perhaps it's maintaining the Easter dinner tradition that your grandparents had started. Whatever your regular sacred time, recognize the healing and restorative power that comes from belonging to a group that values and loves you.

7. **Share your successes.** Many successful individuals go to the opposite extreme of becoming haughty. Instead of feeling superior to their families, they remain humble and modestly resist sharing their successes. They may fear being ostracized and misunderstood by those who do not have a context for appreciating the new account they've won or the grad school acceptance letter they've just received. Most families, however, want to celebrate with you and will appreciate the opportunity to be close to you. Your spirit of humility can still prevail even as you call Aunt Gladys and tell her about your promotion. Let the

family know how much their support, encouraging words, and examples of hard work have meant to your success.

Patchwork Progress

The other valuable lesson I mentioned gleaning from Walker's story "Everyday Use" is no less important than remembering where you come from. You know, the great thing about quilts is not the ornate colorful pattern we see on the front. Nor is it merely the warmth that's intrinsic to every loving stitch. No, the real beauty lies in understanding that the elegance of the concept is heightened by the mixing of different textures. Think about the way quilts bring together fabrics that would otherwise never have touched. They're different, but that's what makes them so special in relation to one another. It's like a family reunion, where the haves and the have-nots all come together to express the common threads of their origins!

Let's examine the idea of the quilt more closely for a moment. One warm luxurious piece of emerald-green velvet (left over from a childhood Christmas dress) is stitched to a nice gray flannel square from Grandpa's old pajama bottoms. I bet he never would have dreamed that his pj's would end up connected to Aunt Mabel's red wool scarf. It all adds up to an ensemble that makes for loving warmth conveyed with resourceful artistry. You can't have the quilt without the contribution of many people's belongings. Some fabrics are ordinary and some exotic, but all are important to making the quilt the wonderful eclectic blanket of life that it's meant to be. There's a patchwork progress in the way garments and pieces of fabric that are no longer useful unto themselves find new life when united with other scraps and tattered pieces of cloth.

Whether quilts or families, what can hold such odd pieces of different shapes and textures together? If you've ever examined one of Grandma's quilts, you know the collection of various and disparate pieces is held together by the stray threads, odd stitching patterns, and knots tied on the back side of the quilted fabrics. Remember that all families have a back side, yours and mine. Do not allow the pain of the past, the contradictions of the present, or the pleasant exposure you've had to nicely packaged people in your new life to alienate you from the "not so nice" side of your natural family, spiritual family, or cultural family. They might not be as luxurious as the upper echelon of society you now rub elbows with, but they are nonetheless a part of the story. Do not allow success to cause you to trade in the lifelong legacy of the hand-me-down quilt for the simulated, factory-produced, digitally enhanced version that has everything going for it except authenticity and loving craftsmanship.

Now, I know the mass-produced quilt has no wild, loose threads. It has no knots tied in the back and it looks first-rate from every angle. But the only reason it looks like that is that it is not a real quilt. For you see, real quilts are made of love and patience. Their beauty on top often helps to camouflage the many mistakes on the back side. Like the long strands of abiding love, they cover sins and overlook mistakes and forgive indiscretions. "Above all, love each other deeply, because love covers over a multitude of sins" (1 Peter 4:8, NIV).

Remaining a part of your family community and giving back to it may require dealing with some wild threads and broken pieces. But "keeping it real" is what makes it beautiful. We have a tendency to want a nice, neat little world that has orderly family members and positive role models. We want a community that is sound and stable, loving and supportive. We would like to see the pleasant, smiling faces of perfect individuals whose flawless manners and impeccable charm always add without taking, give without asking. But because we ourselves will never reach that state completely, we would benefit more from seeing how the back side relates to the top side. The crucial flaw of the factory-produced quilt is that it doesn't show us how to keep the pieces together in this imperfect world we live in. It suggests that all sides of all pieces are perfectly made to form nice, identical rectangles. It simply isn't so. What we really need is to hear from broken, fallible, flawed people who made it in spite of the back side of life. We need to see the threads underneath to know that it's possible to have known a rough past and still have the prospect of a beautiful future.

No matter who we are or where we come from, isn't the necessity of love and forgiveness the true essence of brotherhood? Don't these threads bind us together—black and white, rich and poor? Isn't this the common thread between the secular and the sacred, the young and the old? We all have a need to supply ourselves certain elements of survival in life—food, water, air, shelter. But we need other people just as much, no matter how independent or self-reliant we may consider ourselves to be. This is the thread that binds our community together, giving us unity in the midst of diversity. It is what unites straights and gays, Democrats and Republicans, red states and blue states, the saints and the sinners, the high school dropouts and the Ivy League Ph.D.s. We are all human beings crafted in the image of our Creator. We don't have to relate to each issue, or agree on every detail, to respect each person. We all meet at the funeral home. We all need to love and be loved. No family is filled with all of one and none of the other. But they are family nonetheless. No community can free itself from all outside influences. You need only look at history to know that all who tried to build their own little utopia cut off from the rest of the world became a cult and eventually self-destructed or were otherwise destroyed. From the disciples' failed attempt to "have all things in common" in the book of Acts to the Guyana debacle, from the KKK in the sixties to Waco, none of us can barricade ourselves in without damaging the whole garment and texture.

We mustn't allow the uniqueness of our particulars to cause us to lose sight of our common desires. Just because we have reached a new level of success, financial solvency, or material blessing, our needs—particularly the intangible needs for love and belonging—do not go away. Who among us doesn't long to be loved and understood on a daily basis? Who among us doesn't want to be accepted or enhanced and inspired by our associations? Many of us have made wrong turns even if we had the right plans. We need both history beneath us and destiny above us to feel sheltered and completed.

Better Than Before

You have extraordinary opportunities before you, possibilities secured by the blood, sweat, tears, and dollars of your parents, grandparents, and their parents. Don't separate yourself from your heritage, be it black, white, Hispanic, Asian, or some other rich ethnicity. Use the quilts that your ancestors patched together from what they had been given. Warm yourself, comfort yourself, and sustain yourself by remembering what came before you. Add your own unique designs to this quilt so that when you pass it on, others will benefit from what you have learned and how you have lived.

Tell your story, show your colors, add your slant to it. Stitch your wisdom in with your grandmother's and pass it on. Your life is part of an intergenerational masterpiece, a quilt of lives linked by more than blood, a tapestry woven from sacrifice, resilience, and triumph. When our children's children receive it, they need to see that we all have a responsibility, not so much to duplicate what our ancestors did but to make our own mark. We must not simply wrap ourselves up in a cocoon of comfort and benefit from the warmth of past generations' labor. We are called to add some new element to the fabrics given to us so that the next generation will know that they, too, have a story to add, a song to sing, a gift to give. Contributing to the community is like adding to the quilt. You leave a memorial behind to let the world know that you were here.

Too many people are interested only in taking what is given them and adding nothing to it. You and I have been given a great gift. Every great-grandma who ever dipped snuff taught us something. Uncle Joe might have been a drunk, but he and Aunt Sissy took in the neighborhood children and loved them as their own. Despite their flaws, they made a difference. Mother couldn't cook so well, but she bought a dress for a needy child who would have gone to the prom in blue jeans had it not been for her godmother's loving kindness! Sadie taught Sunday school and Mr. Fred started a Boy Scout troop. Doesn't sound like much until you stitch it all together. The silent gifts and untold sacrifices to give something back, to love someone just as much as you love yourself. When you add them all together, they form the unity hidden in community, the binding agent of benevolence, the glue of generosity.

You cannot have community without unity. The greatest challenge is to take people who have so much to divide them and find a reason to unite them. Yes, life can be cold and there are plenty of moments when we can choose to become as cold as the harsh life we've experienced. But if you are wise, if you are really pursuing a life of balanced prosperity in all areas, then you will fight off the chilled arctic air of struggle and disappointment with the warm relentless love that gives something back. You have been given so you can give. Don't apologize for what you have been given, just always remember to add something to it and give something back.

Your quilt may look neat and orderly, with beautiful stitches and an even pattern of remembrance, but for most of us, I believe it will look more like a crazy quilt, a haphazard, beautiful conglomeration of different fabrics, textures, and patterns. It may have started out as a wedding-ring pattern or starburst but now resembles an explosion of red, blue, green, plaid, polka dots, calico, and madras. Just as others before you have repositioned themselves and made the family quilt their own, you can change the pattern as well.

No matter what it may look like, draw strength from it—others before you likely endured trials just as harsh as, or worse than, those you may be facing now. If they can make it, so can you. Their triumphs are yours as well, just as your success provides a new design for future generations. Finally, cherish the quilt for what it is: a souvenir of your past, a foundation for your present, and a bridge to the future!

Much Is Required

Whoever finds his life will lose it, and whoever loses his
life for my sake will find it.
—*Matthew 10:39 (NIV)*

My first trip to Nigeria is indelibly engraved upon my memory
for many reasons. I instinctively found myself drawn to the
amazing people, art, culture, music, and food of this beautiful African country—and no wonder, as I have since learned that this was
the homeland of my ancestors. The city of Lagos reminded me of
any large, growing urban hub, with skyscrapers dimly lighting the
night sky and ongoing construction camouflaging the homeless
hidden among more prosperous abodes.

Perhaps the most memorable event of my visit occurred as I
walked down the street with a group of Nigerian pastors. A handful of children scurried after us, clustering around me in my American suit as a potential benefactor. Embedded in their dark faces

were lines of poverty, fear, and hunger, features expressing a lost innocence that no child should have to experience. As I began to dig in my pocket for whatever cash I had on hand, more children seemed to materialize out of the shadowed alleys with their small hands extended toward me. I passed out bills and coins to each one, and I assumed that we would continue on our way. My Nigerian hosts, however, were chuckling at me, and while I wasn't offended, I did think it a bit strange and assumed I was committing some kind of cultural faux pas.

I filled what I perceived to be the last child's hand and realized that several dozen more children now encircled me. Several were paraplegic, positioned on skateboards to enable them to move. More were lining up behind us, from those barely able to toddle down the sidewalk to others approaching their early teens. Some were clearly suffering some illness or injury, along with malnutrition. Tears brimmed in my eyes at such a sight, and I quickly dug in my pockets for every last cent and dollar I could find. I hated that I did not have more cash with me and wondered how I could partner with the Nigerian churches I'd be visiting to meet the needs of this large group of suffering children.

As the crowd of children dissipated and my hosts and I were once more alone, I couldn't help but notice that their polite chuckles had erupted into full-blown laughter. I was now getting a bit upset that a sight that moved my heart so forcefully should have precipitated laughter in those closest to the situation. So, of course, I had to inquire: "Please tell me what's so funny."

"You are a generous and compassionate man, Bishop Jakes," said one of the Nigerians. "But you must realize that there is no way you can meet the needs of every child here in Lagos. We do all what we can, but yet the poor seem to multiply more than any ministry or philanthropy can keep up with. We laugh only because your compassionate donations to these young ones could go on forever."

I instantly knew what he was talking about and realized that I had just experienced a variation of one of our church's largest problems: how to focus our resources to help those who need it most. You also will, and no doubt already have, felt the burn of trying to respond to everyone's need. You don't have to run a ministry or manage a company to become overwhelmed by needs and have to accept your inability to meet everyone's. As we begin this last chapter, I believe it is essential that as we become more and more successful, we give back to our communities. But I also know how challenging, draining, and even discouraging it can be when you're giving all you can only to be criticized for missing the needs of others. Whether you are a mother stressed with endless demands of insensitive children, or a young man who always gets called to help friends and family, we all have people who want more from us than we have left to give. Working women know all too well that sometimes they cannot be great cooks, sharp businesswomen, fundraisers for the ladies' lodge, and regular stay-fit members of the gym. It's hard to wear a teddy for Freddy at midnight and still have on your navy-blue suit for the 7 AM breakfast meeting! Giving may imbue you with a warm feeling of gratification, but it can quickly turn into heartburn when you realize that there is no end to the line of people who want your wares and will quickly attack you when you run out before they are finished with you. As CeCe Winans sings so beautifully in "Alabaster Box," "No one knows the cost of the oil in my alabaster box!" It costs you so much more than finances to be a giver.

The Price of Giving

While he was in Bethany, reclining at the table in the home of a man known as Simon the Leper, a woman came with an alabaster jar of very expensive perfume, made of pure nard. She broke the jar and poured the perfume on his head.

Some of those present were saying indignantly to one another, "Why this waste of perfume? It could have been sold for more than a year's wages and the money given to the poor." And they rebuked her harshly.

"Leave her alone," said Jesus. "Why are you bothering her? She has done a beautiful thing to me. The poor you will always have with you, and you can help them any time you want. But you will not always have me. She did what she could. She poured perfume on my body beforehand to prepare for my burial."

—*Mark 14:3–8 (NIV)*

My experience with the Nigerian children and the words of my host remind me of this exchange between Jesus and his disciples. Even his own followers were critical of the gift that this woman presented to their Master. But Jesus turns their rebuke of her back on them, admonishing them to leave her alone and making a very surprising, but oh-so-true observation in defense of her gift. "The poor you will always have with you, and you can help them any time you want," He says. "But you will not always have me."

The challenge that we have faced at the Potter's House is one that every church, ministry, philanthropy, charitable organization, and compassionate individual faces: how to choose which needs to address and how to allocate resources to meet those needs. For many years, our church focused on meeting the needs of the homeless. We not only organized shelters and job fairs but held large celebrations where food was bountiful, clothes were provided, and gifts for the children were available. By all accounts the events were successful, but soon we faced criticism that we needed to do more to encourage family bonds, particularly with males in our community. So we began hosting father-son outings, followed by father-daughter outings.

What happened next? You guessed it—women requested that we do more for them, for the single mothers and for the elderly. We experienced a similar snowball effect when we began digging wells in African villages to provide fresh water for the people there. Soon other international needs became known—in Mexico, South America, South Africa, the Far East. It was like trying to paint the Golden Gate Bridge—just as we finally completed the massive project, we needed to start it all over again. It seemed endless, and despite the good we were doing, the many lives we were saving and improving, others continued to criticize us for not doing more.

Give to Receive

I believe that in order to be truly and fully successful you must give back to those in need around you. If you want to reposition yourself for ongoing and sustained success, then you must incorporate a generous and compassionate spirit in your equation. However, you must also realize that the needs of this world are insatiable.

> The horseleach hath two daughters, crying, Give, give. There are three things that are never satisfied, yea, four things say not, It is enough: The grave; and the barren womb; the earth that is not filled with water; and the fire that saith not, It is enough.
>
> Proverbs 30:14–15 (KJV)

Like the appetite of a fire or that of the ocean, the needs of those around us are indeed limitless. A fire never reaches a limit where it has burned enough and will automatically extinguish itself. The ocean never reaches the brim of some invisible container and refuses to spill over into a mighty flood. No matter how wealthy, talented, resourceful, or compassionate one may be, you can never rid the world of all the hurting, hungry, homeless, helpless people it contains. There are simply too many important causes to ever eliminate them all. From AIDS and HIV to breast cancer, from Alzheimer's to arthritis, from illiteracy to Parkinson's, from victims of a tsunami to those displaced by Katrina, on and on the list goes. Just as one disease, disorder, or disturbance disappears, five more emerge to replace it.

Such inexhaustibility does not absolve us from the need to give, as some might maintain. And it can be tempting to think, "What difference can my meager contribution make? I'm only one person." But it's the cumulative effect of all of us giving that provides hope, healing, and help for everyone, not just the ones in need. For we are all touched by need, if not directly in the present, then through those we love in the past or the future. We are compelled to give in order to know the fullness of what it means to prosper. Like the tree that replenishes the forest with its seeds, we must thrive not just for our own comfort or convenience but for the well-being of all around us.

Part of the reason that the Lord blesses us is so we can bless others. Consider Joseph, for instance. Condemned to captivity and thrown into prison, he was then released and became the prime minister in Egypt. He knows he has a responsibility to give something back and now worries about his family back in Israel, yearning to be reunited with his brothers despite how they treated him. He is no doubt the blessed one. And out of that blessing comes a responsibility. He makes sure that his family has the food they need in the midst of a terrible famine throughout the land.

To him to whom much is given, much is required. I believe that those who are blessed have a responsibility to help the oppressed; that is not to say that this responsibility relieves the victim of his responsibility to be a good steward of those opportunities. But the fact is that both the brother who succeeds and the brothers who await success are mutually liable. If we do not create an effective brotherhood that transcends our differences and focuses on our commonalities, then we will never know true joy and contentment.

As a leader, I have given much thought to this issue. I feel that even in the church world, churches that have more must do more. Success is not given in order to intimidate the oppressed, nor can it be maintained if we only act as enablers to the needy, perpetuating their problems without demanding responsibility on their part. Peter and John took the lame man by the hand, but the lame man still had to do some leaping. Peter had the faith to raise him, but the man needed to have the desire to leap.

Today, some would have us think that those who succeed must do it all, when in fact both the giver and the receiver have to accept each other's commitment to betterment. What's the old saying? Give a man a fish, and you feed him for a day. Teach a man to fish, and you feed him for a lifetime. We must empower those struggling behind us to catch up and experience the same level of prosperity that we now enjoy. This is the best gift we can give to those in need—education, information, and mentoring. If we provide only dollars and donations, then we're basically instituting a new welfare system that enables rather than empowers. None of us benefits in such cases.

Social advocacy without social responsibility produces affirmative action for students who still won't go to school. It provides first-time home ownership for people who refuse to stop renting. It attempts to provide welfare as a bridge but becomes a crutch. Joseph helped his brothers, but he didn't carry them. The principle of giving back is a very significant one, and not only for the recipient. Sharing the blessings that the Lord has bestowed upon you is one of the privileges that distinguishes the benefactor from the beneficiary. It's a way of announcing to oneself that one is healed enough to help.

This is an important declaration of independence and a vital sign of recovery. Much like a doctor will not release a patient from the hospital until her vital signs have been restored and she is able to get around on her own, we must show evidence that we are productive by our contribution. This causes a recycling of strengths and replicates within our community what nature teaches. Every plant gives back seed to the ground; likewise, all of us are not truly prosperous until we have enough to give something back.

We are not interested in mere survival; we want success. Success is attained when there is overflow, which is simply another way of describing profit. How do we overflow? We do it through charitable donations, we do it through compassionate acts of kindness, and we do it through service to those less fortunate. Now, I must warn you that people will always demand more, but this is not about the incessant demands of people; as Jesus so aptly put it, the poor you have with you always. This is not about the latest cause that uses guilt to fund-raise. This is about a personal awareness of your responsibility to give back to the soil out of which you've grown and flourished. This is about having the strength of character to choose the causes that you are most passionate about and to let the criticism of others roll off your back.

Repositioned to Thrive

As our time together in these pages comes to a conclusion, I pray that you have much to give back because of the success that you are enjoying in your life. My hope is that you close this book inspired, encouraged, and better equipped to reposition yourself for a life you've only dreamed about. So many forces and factors in our lives can inhibit us, thwart us, and slow down our progress toward prosperity.

We must remain vigilant as we move forward, learning from our past mistakes and forgiving ourselves for yesterday's failures. We must remain true to ourselves and our heart's dreams, never settling for less than our full potential. Finally, we must look beyond our current definitions of success and ensure that our lives are balanced with blessings beyond career, work, and finances.

You must remember that no matter where you are, it's not too late to start over, begin anew, or grow to a higher level. You have everything you need to reposition yourself, to throw off the limitations of others, and to thrive. Like a mighty oak or a beautiful rose, you are destined for greatness, growing taller into maturity, flourishing with an inner beauty yet to be released. Go forward, my brothers and sisters, and get started—your life without limits awaits!

Acknowledgments

You cannot reposition yourself without the support, encouragement, and commitment of those around you, sharing a vision of who you are and where you are going. Similarly, an endeavor of this magnitude was only accomplished through the many contributions of those around me who know me and share my desire to touch as many lives as possible with this urgent message. This book has ripened not only as the fruit of my vision and labor, but through the investment of so many individuals who worked alongside me. Without the many gifted people who keep me on track and on time, I would not be able to attempt fulfilling so many diverse aspirations.

I'm thrilled to be working with my new publishing family at Atria Books and so grateful for their tireless efforts to make this project exceed all our expectations. I'm indebted to Judith Curr, Carolyn Reidy, Gary Urda, and Christine Saunders for making me feel so welcome and catching the vision for this book. To Michael Selleck and Larry Norton, your hard work on behalf of this project is appreciated more than you know. Sue Fleming, thank you for your powerful contribution.

My thanks to Malaika Adero for her editorial dexterity and enhancement of my rather unique way with words on these pages. I'm grateful to Dudley Delffs for sharing his expertise and for allowing me to bounce my ideas off him.

My deep and abiding gratitude goes out to Jan Miller and Shannon Marven at Dupree, Miller, & Associates. Jan, your belief in me and vision for where we can take my message continues to amaze me. Thank you for your passion and commitment to excellence on my behalf. Shannon, your tireless efforts and positive problem solving made such a difference here. My sincerest thanks to you both.

Finally, my ongoing gratitude flows from the wellspring of support provided by my wife and children. Serita, you have shared in this journey with me and repositioned yourself as needed to fulfill your destiny as a strong, beautiful woman whose compassionate heart touches many lives but none more than my life and that of our children. Thank you for being there and seeing who I am and where we are going. The journey continues!

Scripture Notes

Chapter 7: Ready, Aim, Fire

115   "I have given you the land": *see* Joshua 1:1–2 (KJV)

Chapter 11: Breaking Glass Ceilings

192   "Or what of the great debate that existed in Jesus' day": John 8:1–11 (KJV)

Chapter 12: Shattering Glass Slippers

204   "But the truth really can set you free": *see* John 8:32

Chapter 14: Flight Manual

236   "Like Jacob and Esau in the Bible who fought each other": *see* Genesis 25:22

243   "When the children of Israel left for the Promised Land": *see* Exodus 13

Chapter 15: Stay Connected

256   "Much like Paul writing to the church at Corinth": *see* 1 Corinthians 12

Epilogue: Much Is Required

270   "Consider Joseph, for instance": *see* Genesis 37–50

271   "To him to whom much is given": *see* Luke 12:48